INTRODUCING
ARABIC

INTRODUCING
ARABIC

MICHAEL MUMISA

Goodword Books

First published 2003
Reprinted 2004
© Goodword Books, 2004

Goodword Books Pvt. Ltd.
1, Nizamuddin West Market
New Delhi 110 013
e-mail: info@goodwordbooks.com
Printed in India

---

www.goodwordbooks.com

To

Shaikh Muhammad Cassim Sema ,
and *Shaikh Musa Ibrahim Menk,*
the founders of the two leading
and oldest centres of advanced Arabic studies
in Southern Africa, for the many decades
spent promoting advanced Arabic studies
in English countries.

To *Khadijah,* for the difficult years
spent on Arabic and to all those studying
and teaching Arabic Language and Literature.

Contents

Preface

The first time I saw Arabic letters and alphabets was when I was seven years old after a visit to the local Mosque with my father. This was on the occasion of the grand opening of the local Mosque. I can vaguely remember previous visits to other Mosques prior to this one but this particular visit is the one that has remained in my memory until now for two reasons. First because at seven years I was old enough to notice and understand what was happening around me, and secondly because this particular visit marked the beginning of my intellectual and spiritual journey. Most of us children present on that day had come because we knew that we would get to see the traditional Sufi rituals of song and dance since almost all our parents belonged to the *qadiriyyah* Sufi order. We also were aware that on occasions such as this one the food was always delicious. While our mothers and sisters were busy preparing the food to be served after the ceremony and rituals, our fathers and brothers were engaged in the decorations of the stage and Mosque as well as other preparations for the invited guests. Shaikh Ali Dawud, my grandfather and the founder of the Mosque, took this opportunity to recruit more children for his Qur'anic Arabic classes. He gathered us all in the female section of the Mosque and handed each one of us with a new *qai'dah* (a traditional text used to teach children Arabic alphabets and Quranic words). When I looked at the pages and saw those strange signs and characters looking back at me, I wondered if I would ever be able to decipher any of them. A strange fear gripped me and I nearly walked out, however, when I heard my three cousins who were the same age as me reciting fluently the alphabets and words, I decided that if they could do it maybe I also could do it. After just a few days of attending the *Kuttab* (traditional Qur'anic school), I could hardly remember that I was the same person who had nearly walked out of the class not so sure if I could be able to learn the Arabic letters.

This problem affects most people who learn Arabic as a second language, and at times even those who are supposed to speak Arabic as their mother tongue since most of today's Arabs have been disengaged from pure Arabic language.

Over the years I have seen the same uncertainty and at times fear in some of the students, mostly adults, and some of them from Arab ethnic backgrounds, when they are trying to study Arabic for the first time. They also admit that they are not so sure that there will ever come a time when they will be able to read the "strange signs" and characters known as Arabic. After a few days of studying and working hard they can hardly recognise their own voices when they are reading fluently, and when the shaky voice is replaced with a steady and confident one.

Generally speaking Arabic language is easy, probably one of the easiest languages to learn. There is always a connection between words and their derivatives and the grammar laws are logical. The problem however is that most of the methods which have been in use over the year to teach Arabic leave a lot to be desired. There is what one may call an obsession and impatience to teach Arabic grammar to people who lack even rudimentary knowledge of basic Arabic sounds and words (*al-aswat wa al-huruf*). The result of this approach is that people are able to memorise complicated Arabic grammar laws and yet they remain unable to construct simple Arabic sentences in speech and writing. I have known renowned Muslim scholars, mostly from South Asia, South East Asia, Iran, and those teaching in the Indo-Pakistan seminaries in the West, who have spent many years of their lives teaching difficult classical Arabic texts and grammar books through their own languages (Urdu,

Persian, English, Bahasa Malay, etc) and yet are unable to speak a few sentences in fluent Arabic or write a simple Arabic letter or paper.

A person needs working knowledge of a language before she can start learning the grammar of that language. When a person is able to read and understand sentences in a given language, it becomes easier to study the grammar of that language. It is difficult enough learning to recognise the Arabic letters and sounds let alone understanding the grammatical concepts of a language which one is not familiar with. There are thus five stages that need to be followed in presenting Arabic to total beginners:

1. The listening stage - مرحلة الســـماع : At this stage all the student has to do is sit and listen to the Arabic sentences, words, their sounds, and meanings. This is the easiest part.

2. The speech stage – مرحلة الكــلام : The student will have subconsciously memorised Arabic sentences, sounds, and meaning after the first stage. It will be easier to teach her to repeat and speak the words and sentences she has already heard many times. This stage will focus on loosening the student's tongue enabling her to pronounce fluently the Arabic letters and words.

3. The reading stage - مرحلة القراءة : After having learnt the Arabic sounds and meanings of words, and how to pronounce them, it becomes easier for a person to learn how to read the language. At this stage all a person has to do is to learn how to relate the sounds and meanings she has learnt to the signs on the page.

4. The writing stage مرحلة الكتابة : – During the writing stage the student starts learning how to construct Arabic sentences. Equipped already with a vocabulary acquired during the listening, speech, and readings stages, the student will have no difficulty at all joining words in an attempt to construct sentences.

5. The stage of grammar laws مرحلــة القواعــد- : Learning grammar laws will be much easier for a person who already knows how to read the language and understands the meaning of sentences. A student at this stage will have no difficulty identifying, say, verbs from nouns or particles since she will already know the meanings of the words.

One common mistake made by some students and teachers of Arabic is to concentrate on memorising single Arabic words in their attempt to build a good vocabulary. This can be a very crippling approach. Since linguists can now agree that it is much more difficult to memorise single words than it is to memorise sentences. Some students are surprised that they are able to memorise hundreds of Arabic words and yet they have problem understanding Arabic speech or written texts. This is because they do not know how to use these words in sentences. However, if one was to learn sentences, she would also be learning how words are used in sentences. Reading an Arabic text would become very easy since a person would be able to understand the meaning of strange words from the context and the way they appear in a given sentence.

Of course some of the above stages we discussed can run concurrently depending on the age of the student and number of students in the class. This is not the place to address, even at rudimentary level, the modern methods of second language acquisition with special reference to Arabic. If God wills, we intend to complete in the near future a separate work that deals with this topic in greater detail.

The decision to prepare this book came after noticing that most of the books available in English are either too difficult for a student to understand because of the Arabic script used as well as the complicated grammar terminologies employed by the authors (some of whom write from a German or French background), or too basic as to cover all the important Arabic grammatical concepts and laws. The latter genre provides working knowledge in what we may call "tourist Arabic" and fails to equip a student with the necessary language skills needed to read and understand classical texts. Moreover, most of the best books available in English are reference texts for serious researchers and academics, most of whom already know Arabic grammar.

The present textbook is an attempt to present in simple language and style some of the basic as well as advanced Arabic grammar laws to the English reader. It is hoped that it will benefit both those who have just been initiated into this very exciting field of Arabic grammar as well as those who are already at an advanced stage of their studies.

The problem that one encounters when writing an Arabic grammar text using English as *metalanguage* is that one is constantly thinking in Arabic and this is always evident in the translations produced as a result of such a process. In this book I have provided a lot of Arabic examples some of which I have translated into English. I have done my best to assure that the translation of all sentences and passages is as closest to the original Arabic as possible and at the same time presented in good English. Arabic is not always an easy language to translate into any language. Therefore, if you come across English sentences that may not be according to "the Queen's standard", just pretend that you are an Arab learning English!

Definition of *Nahw*:

The technical term used in Arabic for grammar is النَّحْوُ (*al-nahw*) which literally means "to intend", "direction", "similar to", "fashion", "mode", "method". According to Arabic legend, it was the Caliph Ali who first used this word after one of his disciples had presented him with a grammar text he had written. Ali is reported to have remarked, "مَا أَحْسَنَ هَذَا النَّحْوَ الَّذِي نَحَــوْتَ!" – *"What a good method this is you have employed!"*. The science of Arabic syntax was thus termed *nahw*. Scholars define *nahw* as "that branch of knowledge which deals with the laws that govern the end-cases of words in a sentence, such as *declension, indeclension*, etc."[1]

When a person is reading this book without a teacher, it is assumed that she already has some basic knowledge of Arabic words, sentences, sounds, and their meaning. Otherwise one would need a teacher to go through this book successfully. The book is divided into twenty two chapters or lessons and each chapter is followed by an exercise. Examples used in this book are taken from the Qur'an, the *hadith,* classical Arabic texts, as well as other sentences used in everyday life. This book is based on three celebrated Arabic classical sources of grammar; *Sharh ibn aqil ala alfiyat ibn Malik* by Abdullah b. Aqil (698-769 A.H), *Awdah al-masalik ila alfiyat ibn Malik* by Abdullah b. Yusuf b. Hisham al-Nahwi, and the *Muqaddimah* of Abu Abdullah b. Muhammad b. Dawud al-Sanhaji (672-723 A.H) well known as Ibn Ajrum. I have deliberately avoided discussing the differences among the various schools of Arabic grammar regarding the explanation of certain laws since this is a subject that can be dealt with at a very advanced stage. Moreover, a

---

[1] Muhyi al-Din Abdul Hamid, M, *Tuhfat al-sunniyah bi sharh al-muqaddimah al-ajrumiyyah,* Cairo: Maktabat al-Sunnah, 1989, p. 4.

student can only appreciate such discussions if she has a good background in Arabic grammar and linguistics.

There are a lot of people who, though they may not have been directly involved, they made it possible for me to complete this book. Among those who contributed to my academic formation, I would like to express my gratitude to my first teacher the late Shaikh Ali Daud, may the Almighty God have mercy upon him, who introduced me to the field of Arabic and Islamic studies while I was just a young boy, but could not live long to see the fruits of his work. My acknowledgement also goes to Shaikh Muhammad Amin Hamandishe, Shaikh Shabir and Musa Menk, Shaikh Umar Phiri, and Shaikh Ibrahim Sumani (a.k.a. *Tarkib Tawsifi*) whose unorthodox methods of teaching grammar laws worked miracles on the students. I remember how, following behind with a stick in his hand, he once made all the grammar students march daily for the whole month in military style through the corridors of Iqra' College chanting "*tarkibu! Tawsifiyyu!*" after they had found it difficult to memorise the law of *tarkib tawsifi*, it was from then onwards that he became known as "Shaikh Tarkib."

I wish, further, to express my appreciation to all the linguists and grammarians at the Dārul Ulūm al-Islāmiyah College at Newcastle (South Africa) with whom I learnt the classical texts of Arabic literature, poetry and prose, Arabic *Rhetorics*, grammar and linguistics; Shaikh Muhammad Cassim Sema, Shaikh Abdul Kader Hoosen, Shaikh Fairuz al-Din Adam, Mufti Fayyaz, and many others who were responsible for my education for the six years I spent studying there. Not forgetting all my Professors at the Rand Afrikaans University as well as those who are assisting me now at the University of Birmingham here in the United Kingdom, and I would like to single out Dr. Jabal Muhammad Buaben who has proved to be both teacher and brother, my supervisor Dr David Thomas, Dr Sigvard von Sicard, and others. I also would like to mention here my friends and brothers; Hasan, Zahir Mahmood, my two cousins Shaikh Tayyib Makwemba and Shaikh Muhammad Milazi in the Faculty of Humanities at the University of Durban-Westville, and others, who, although not aware of it, were a great inspiration to my work.

I have benefited greatly from the comments and criticisms of others. Sister Mahdiyyah of London read most or all of the manuscript and made valuable remarks.

I must also mention here Mrs Salma Zishan for the many hours she spent on the computer typing and preparing the manuscript for the publisher. The following people were also very helpful in different ways: Shaikh Muhammad Amin-Evans, Shaikh Arif A Hussein, Shauqat al-Najafi, Mahmood Dhalla, J.K. Simatei, and others.

As far as the publication of this book is concerned, it affords me great pleasure to record my sincere gratitude to Saniyasnain Khan and Goodword Books who agreed to publish this book and without whose support this book would not have materialised.

Michael Mumisa

Birmingham, UK
January 2003

Chapter One

الكَلَامُ العَرَبِيّ : الاسمُ و الفِعْلُ و الحَرْفُ

The concept of speech in Arabic grammar: The Noun, The verb, and The Particle

The word الكَلَامُ (*al- kalām*) in Arabic literally means "speech". It is used by scholars of Arabic language to denote meaningful speech, or what they call الكَلَامُ المُفِيْدُ (*al-kalām al-mufīd*). In other words, if words come out of a person's mouth, they must make sense in order for them to be classified as *kalām*.

They go on to divide *kalām* into two categories:

1. Verbal speech   –   الكَلَامُ اللَّفْظِيُّ
2. Non-verbal speech – الكَلَامُ غَيْرُ اللَّفْظِيِّ

So far the meaning of *kalām* we have discussed above is according to the scholars of Arabic linguistics and not according to the scholars of Arabic grammar. The Arabic grammarians have a very restricted meaning of *kalām*. According to them anything we call speech must fulfil four conditions:

1 It must be verbal speech. This means that it must be based on Arabic alphabets and sounds, e.g. words such as كِتَابٌ (a book), قَلَمٌ (a pen), يَذْهَبُ (he is going). The reason for putting this condition is because Arabic grammar seeks to analyse words and how they are used in sentences, with a focus on the last letter in a word (or what is known as an

end-case). This can only be possible if speech is verbal. Sign language therefore, as well as all other forms of non-verbal communication, is not speech according to Arabic grammarians since one cannot grammatically analyse sign language.

2. It must be a combination of two or more words - المُرَكَّبُ. For example:

الكِتابُ جَدِيْدٌ — The book is new.

يَذْهَبُ زَيْدٌ إلى السُّوْقِ — Zaid is going to the market.

This is mainly because in Arabic language complete and meaningful sentences are made up of two or more words and never a single word. However, if you were asked a question in Arabic such as, مَــنْ أُخْتُــكِ؟ -"who is your sister?" and you answered, فَاطِمَــة -"Fatimah", the Arabic grammarians would consider this single word (Fatimah) as *kalām* since it is understood from the very situation of dialogue that you are saying, فَاطِمَةُ أُخْتِي "Fatima is my sister." It is important to note here that Grammar scholars refer to the combination of two or more words as المُرَكَّبُ (al-murakkab), which when literally translated into English means "composite". They go on to divide المُرَكَّبُ into two categories:

a) Meaningful composite المُرَكَّبُ المُفِيد (*al-murakkab al-mufīd*), e.g. زَيْدٌ قَائِمٌ (Zaid is standing)

b) Unmeangiful composite المُرَكَّبُ غَيرَ المُفِيد (*al-murakkab ghair al- mufīd*), e.g. كِتَابُ زَيْدٍ (Zaid's book).

When grammar scholars speak of *kalām,* they are referring to المُرَكَّبُ المُفِيدُ (meaningful composite) and not غَير المُرَكَّبُ المُفِيدِ (unmeaningful composite).

18

3. The third condition of speech in Arabic grammar is that it must be meaningful (*mufīd*). Suppose if one was to say, كِتَابُ زَيْـــدٍ (Zaid's book), this would not be considered *kalām* although it is a combination of two words. This is mainly because when you hear someone saying "Zaid's book" you are left wondering and asking yourself, "what about Zaid's book? What does he mean by Zaid's book?" The purpose of speech, which is to convey a message that makes sense, is not fulfilled. However, if I was to say, كِتَابُ زَيْدٍ جَدِيْدٌ (Zaid's book is new), this would be a complete and meaningful sentence which the Arabic grammarians would be happy to classify as *kalām*.

4. The final condition is that it must be made up of Arabic words. If it is made up of non-Arabic words then it will not be classified as *kalām* since the laws of Arabic grammar are designed to study Arabic words. This does not mean that grammar scholars do not consider other languages as speech in the linguistic sense, it is simply because Arabic grammar is not equipped to analyse foreign words, just as it is not equipped to analyse non-verbal means of communication, and sign language.

There are three parts of speech in Arabic:

إِسْمٌ - Noun

فِعْلٌ - Verb

حَرْفٌ - Particle

1. The term إِسْمٌ – Noun in Arabic grammar is used to denote things that can be perceived by the senses or understood. The classical books of Arabic grammar would define a noun as "a word that refers to a meaning without being restricted by time." In other words, the meaning of such a word will not be bound by any tense such as past, present, or future tense. The examples of إِسْمٌ - Noun are:

كِتَابٌ	A book
قَلَمٌ	A pen
مَكْتَبٌ	A desk
كُرْسِيٌّ	A chair
مُحَمَّدٌ	Muhammad
فَاطِمَةُ	Fatima
عِلْمٌ	Knowledge
جَهْلٌ	Ignorance
إِيْمَانٌ	Faith/Belief
ظُلْمٌ	Oppression

If you look at the above words you will see that they all have meanings which *signify* objects or entities without being limited by any tense. The word "chair" in the above example is a noun (*al-ism*) referring to an object made from wood or other materials, with a rest for the back, and used as a separate seat for one person. In Arabic linguistics, *al-musammā* (referent, or signified) is the term used for the object or entity referred to, symbolised by, or qualified by a word. You will also see that the word and meaning referring to the *referent* or *signified* (the object we call chair) in our example is not attached to any tense. One cannot speak of a present tense or past tense for the word "chair".

The Characteristics of إسمٌ

The question that a beginner in Arabic studies, or even an Arab who has not had the opportunity to study Arabic grammar, may have is how to identify Arabic nouns and distinguish them from verbs or particles? The following are the characteristics that will help in identifying nouns:

a) A noun accepts a *kasrah* or vowel " i" as an end-case, and this is indicated by the stroke ―― under the last letter of the word, e.g.:

I passed by Zaid.	زَيدٍ: مَرَرْتُ بِزَيْدٍ
This is Muhammad's house.	مُحَمَّدٍ: هَذَا بَيْتُ محمدٍ
The ruler is on the desk.	المَكْتَب: المِسطَرَةُ عَلَى المَكْتَب
Mariam went to the university.	الجَامِعَةِ: ذَهَبَتْ مَريَم إلَى الجَامِعَةِ

The underlined words are all nouns (أَسْمَاء, plural of إسمٌ) since they accept *kasrah* as an end case.

b) A noun will also accept a *tanwin* or nunation on the last letter. A nunation is an "unvowelled" and "unwritten" letter ن (*nun*) and is indicated by the duplication of the final vowel in the word and appears as double vowels ―――― on the last letter of a word. For example:

كِتَابٌ   كِتَاباً   كِتَابٍ

We will discuss this further in chapter four of this book.

c) A noun will also accept ال, the *definite article* which indicates that a noun is definite, e.g.

قَلَمٌ :	A pen.	القَلَمُ	The pen.
رَجُلٌ :	A man	الرَّجُل	The man
بِنْتٌ :	A girl.	البِنْتُ	The girl.
سَيَّارَةٌ :	A car	السَّيَّارَةُ	The car.
إِمْرَأَةٌ :	A woman.	المَرْأَةُ	The woman.

This topic has been discussed in detail in chapter four.

d) A noun will also accept prepositions, e.g.

مِن : مِنَ البَيْتِ	<u>from</u> the house
إِلَى : إِلَى المَسْجِدِ	<u>to</u> the Mosque
عَلَى : عَلَى المَكْتَب	<u>on</u> the desk
فِي : فِي الفَصْلِ	<u>in</u> the classroom

2. The فِعْلٌ - Verb is a word that denotes the occurrence of an action, the meaning of such a word will fall into any one of the three tenses. There are thus three types of verbs:

a) الفِعْلُ الماضي the past tense verb e.g.

كَتَبَ   He wrote.

b) الفِعْلُ المُضَارِعُ the present tense verb e.g.

يَكْتُبُ   He is writing.

c) الفِعْلُ الأَمْرُ the imperative verb e.g. أُكْتُبْ Write!

The following table provides examples of the three types of verbs:

Imperative – الفِعْلُ الأمْرُ	Present tense – الفِعْلُ المُضَارِعُ	Past tense - الفِعْلُ المَاضِي
إذْهَبْ Go	يَذْهَبُ He is going	ذَهَبَ He went
أُكْتُبْ Write	يَكْتُبُ He is writing	كَتَبَ He wrote
أُنصُرْ Help	يَنْصُرُ He is helping	نَصَرَ He helped
إضْرِبْ Hit	يَضْرِبُ He is hitting	ضَرَبَ He hit
إسْمَعْ Hear	يَسْمَعُ He is hearing	سَمِعَ He heard
إقْرَأ Read	يَقْرَأُ He is reading	قَرَأَ He read
قُلْ Say	يَقُوْلُ He is saying	قَالَ He said
إرْضَ Be pleased	يَرْضَى He is pleased	رَضِيَ was pleased
إجْلِسْ Sit	يَجْلِسُ He is sitting	جَلَسَ He sat
أُصْدُقْ Say the truth	يَصْدُقُ He is saying the truth	صَدَقَ He said the truth

The Characteristics of فِعْلٌ:

There are four main features that help us identify a verb in Arabic. Whenever any of these four appear before a word, we will be able to identify that word as a verb:

The believers have achieved salvation.	قَدْ : قَدْ أَفْلَحَ الْمُؤْمِنُونَ
The foolish among people will say...	س : سَيَقُولُ السُّفَهَاءُ مِنَ النَّاسِ
Soon He shall grant them their reward	سَوف : سَوف يُؤْتِيهِم أُجُورَهُمْ
When the wife of Pharaoh said...	ت: اذ قَالَتْ امرَأَةُ فِرْعَونَ

3. The حَرْفٌ or particle is a word which is dependent on the noun or verb in order to convey a complete or useful meaning. Its meaning will be complete when it is used along with the noun or verb in a sentence. e.g.

مِنْ from: خَدِيجَةٌ مِنْ أَفْرِيقِيا
Khadijah is from Africa

إِلَى to/towards: ذَهَبَ زَيْدٌ اِلَى السُّوقِ
Zaid went to the market

عَلَى on/upon : الكِتَابُ عَلَى المَكْتَبِ
The book is on the desk

بِ with/by: يَكْتُبُ الأُسْتَاذُ رِسَالَةً بِالْقَلَمِ
The teacher is writing a letter with a pen

وَ and: اَلْقَلَمُ وَالْكِتَابُ عَلَى المَكْتَبِ
The pen and book are on the desk

According to Muhammad Muhyi al-Din Abdul Hamid, commentator of the celebrated classical grammar text *al-Muqaddima al-ajrumiyyah* of Abu Abdullah bin Muhammad bin Dawud al-Sanhaji well known as Ibn Ajrum (672-723 A.H), "what distinguishes the

24

particle from its cognates; the noun and the verb is that neither the characteristics of the nouns previously discussed nor those of the verbs can be applied to it (the حَرْف) e.g. مِنْ هَلْ لَمْ. These words are examples of particles since they will not accept the *definitive article* (the lettersال), nunation, or prepositions. It will not be correct to say: إِلَى مِنْ – مِنٌّ – الْمِنْ- ..."[1]

The types of sentences in Arabic:

The Arabic sentence is referred to as الجُمْلَة (*al-jumlah*). It refers to a group of no less than two words grouped together to convey a meaning. The sentence commencing with a noun or إِسْمٌ, is termed الجُمْلَةُ الاسْمِيَّةُ (*al-jumlat al-ismiyyah*) or "the nominal sentence." The sentence commencing with a verb or فِعْلٌ is termed الجُمْلَةُ الفِعْلِيَّةُ (*al-jumlat al-fi'liyyah*) or "the verbal sentence". There are thus two types of sentences: nominal إِسْمِيَّةٌ, and verbal فِعليَّةٌ. In order to determine the type of sentence in the case of sentences that commence with the حَرْف or particle, the word appearing immediately after the حَرْف is considered. If the word appearing immediately after the particle is a verb the sentence will be classified as a verbal sentence, and if it is a noun the sentence will be classified as a nominal sentences. The following are examples of nominal and verbal sentences:

البَيْتُ جَمِيلٌ	The house is beautiful. (Nominal)
العِلمُ نَافِعٌ	Knowledge is beneficial. (Nominal)

---

[1] Muhyi al-Din Abdul Hamid, M, *Tuhfat al-suniyyah bi sharh al-muqaddimah al-ajrumiyyah,* Cairo: Maktabat al-Sunnah, 1989, pp.12-13.

المَرْأَةُ ذَكِيَّةٌ   The woman is intelligent. (Nominal)

قَرَأَ الطَّالِبُ الكِتَابَ   The student read the book. (Verbal)

يَأْكُلُ زَيدٌ خُبْزاً   Zaid is eating bread. (Verbal)

أُكْتُبِ الدَّرْسَ   Write the lesson. (Verbal)

هَلِ الأُسْتَاذُ مَوجُودٌ؟   Is the Professor present? (Nominal)

هَلْ ذَهَبَ التَّاجِرُ إِلَى السُّوق

Did the trader go to the market? (Verbal)

قُلْ هُو اللهُ أَحَدٌ   Say He is Allah the one! (Verbal)

الدَّرسُ صَعْبٌ   The lesson is difficult. (Nominal)

القُرْآنُ كِتَابُ الله   The Qur'an is the Book of Allah. (Nominal)

كَسَرَ إِبْرَاهِيمُ الأَصْنَامَ   Ibrahim broke the idols. (Verbal)

SUMMARY

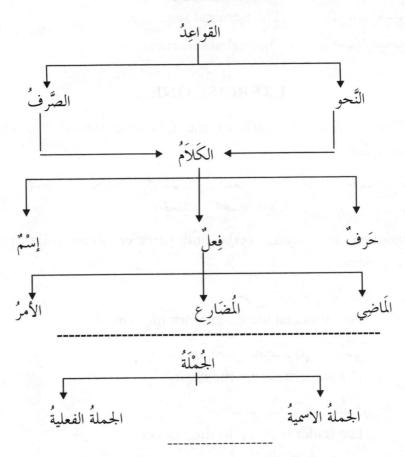

IMPORTANT TERMS

1- الكَلاَمُ   - The word.
2- الاسْمُ   - The noun.
3- الفِعْلُ   - The verb.
4- الفِعْلُ الماضي   - The past tense verb.
5- الفِعْلُ المُضَارِعُ - The present tense verb.

6- الفِعْلُ الأَمْرُ   - The imperative verb.

7- الاسْمِيَّةُ الجُمْلَةُ   - The nominal sentence.

8- الجُمْلَةُ الفِعلية   - The verbal sentence.

EXERCISE ONE

1- What is meant by each of the following terms? Provide examples:

النحو   الكلام   الاسم   الفعل   الحرف   الجملة الاسمية

الجملة   الجملة الفعلية

2- Underline the nouns, verbs and particles in the following examples:

a)   خَرَجَ المُدِيرُ مِن المَدْرَسَةِ

The principal went out from the school.

b)   جَلَسَ الطَّالِبُ علَى الكُرْسِيِّ

The student sat on the chair.

c)   التَاجِرُ يَذْهَبُ إلَى السُوق

The trader is going to the market.

d)   زَيْنَبُ مِنْ لَنْدَن

Zainab is from London.

e)   العَرَبِيَّةُ لُغَةٌ جَمِيْلَةٌ

Arabic is a beautiful language.

f)   ذَهَبَتْ خَدِيجَةُ إلَى الجَامِعَةِ

Khadijah went to the university.

g)   إقْرَأ باسْمِ رَبِّكَ

Read in the name of your Lord!

3. State which of the above sentences are nominal and which are verbal.

4. State which of the following verbs are in the past tense, which are present tense, and which are imperative verbs:

جَلَسَ	نَصَرَ
أَفْلَحَ	صَدَقَ
خَرَجَ	قَالَ
يَذْهَبُ	رَضِيَ
يَكْتُبُ	أُصْدُقْ
يَنْصُرُ	قُلْ
يَضْرِبُ	إِرْضَ
يَسْمَعُ	إِجْلِسْ
يَصْدُقُ	إِقْرَأْ
يَقُولُ	أُكْتُبْ
إذْهَبْ	يَرْضَى
أُنْصُرْ	يَجْلِسُ
إِضْرِبْ	يَقْرَأُ
إِسْمَعْ	كَتَبَ

5- Translate the following sentences into Arabic:

a)   Zainab went to the market.

b)   Zaid is helping Fatima.

c)   Go to the university.

d)   The trader is going to London

e)   Read the book and write the lesson.

Chapter Two

الفَاعِلُ و المَفْعُولُ ـ المُبْتَدَأ و الخَبَرُ

The Subject, the Predicate –
The Doer, the Direct Object

In chapter one, we mentioned that one of the conditions of *kalām* is that it must be المُرَكَّبُ المُفِيْدُ (meaningful composition). We then went on to divide المُرَكَّبُ المُفِيْدُ into two types of sentences: the nominal sentence (الجُمْلَةُ الاسْمِيَّةُ) and the verbal sentence (الجُمْلَةُ الفِعليةُ). In this chapter we will discuss the various parts that make up sentences. In Arabic a sentence is either made up of the subject, known in Arabic as المُبْتَدَأ (*al-mubtada'*) and the predicate or الخَبَرُ (*al-khabar*), or it can also be made up of the verb, the doer of the verb known in grammar as الفَاعِلُ (*al-fā'il*), and the direct object or المَفْعُولُ (*al-maf'ul*).

The Subject المُبْتَدَأ:

The first noun in a nominal sentence is referred to as المُبْتَدَأ or the subject, e.g.

حَامِدٌ مَسْرُورٌ	<u>Hamid</u> is happy
الحَمْدُ لله	<u>All praise</u> belongs to Allah
زَيْدٌ قَائِمٌ	<u>Zaid</u> is standing
الله رَبُّنَا	<u>Allah</u> is our Lord.
مَرْيَمُ تَذهَبُ إِلَى الدُّكَّانِ	<u>Mariam</u> is going to the shop.

القَلَمُ جَدِيْدٌ	<u>The pen</u> is new.
الطِّفْلُ ذَكِيٌّ	<u>The child</u> is intelligent.
البَيْتُ نَظِيْفٌ	<u>The house</u> is clean.

Each of the underlined words in the above examples is a subject or المبتدأ. The subject must always be a noun. A verb or particle can never be a subject. This means therefore that the law of *al-mubtada'* (subject) and *al-khabar* (predicate) is only applicable to nominal sentences and not verbal sentences since we defined nominal sentences in chapter one as those sentences beginning with a noun.

The Predicate الخَبَرُ :

In Arabic the word الخَـــبَـــرُ literally means "news" or "information." The part of the sentence appearing after the subject is called الخَـــبَـــرُ or the predicate. It is the part of the sentence that provides us with more information and news about the subject. e.g.

Praise <u>is due to Allah</u>	الحَمْدُ لله
Zaid <u>is standing</u>	زَيْدٌ قَائِمٌ
Allah <u>is our Lord</u>.	اللهُ رَبُّنَا
Mariam <u>is going to the shop</u>.	مَرْيَم تَذْهَبُ إِلَى الدُّكَّان
The pen <u>is new</u>.	القَلَمُ جَدِيْدٌ
The child <u>is intelligent</u>.	الطِّفْلُ ذَكِيٌّ
The house <u>is clean</u>.	البَيْتُ نَظِيْفٌ

The underlined words in the above examples are predicates (sing. الخَـــبَـــر) . They provide us with information regarding the

31

nouns at the beginning of the sentences. If a speaker was to simply say, الطِّفْــــلُ "The child", we would be left in need of more news and information regarding the child. The word الطِّفْـلُ on its own would not make any sense to us until something was said about the child. The word ذَّكِــيٌّ "intelligent" which comes after الطِّفْــلُ provides us with the information or *khabar* we need to understand the intention of the speaker. Therefore, in a nominal sentence, the subject and predicate together are always needed in order to form a complete sentence e.g.

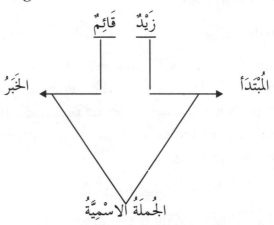

We said that the subject must always be a noun and that a verb cannot be a subject. This law does not apply to the predicate. The predicate can either be a noun or a verb, in some cases it can also be a whole sentence. However, the predicate must concord with the subject in end-case and gender e.g.

مُحَمَّدٌ مُجْتَهِدٌ	Muhammad is hardworking.
فَاطِمَةُ مُجْتَهِدَةٌ	Fatima is hardworking
يُوسُفُ جَمِيْلٌ	Yusuf is handsome

32

خَدِيْجَةٌ جَمِيْلَةٌ	Khadijah is beautiful
الرَّجُلاَنِ قَائِمَانِ	The two men are standing
البِنْتَانِ قَائِمَتَانِ	The two girls are standing
الرِّجَالُ قَائِمُوْنَ	The men are standing
النِّسَاءُ قَائِمَاتٌ	The women are standing
القَلَمُ جَدِيْدٌ	The pen is new
القَلَمَانِ جَدِيْدَانِ	The two pens are new
الأَقْلاَمُ جَدِيْدَةٌ	The pens are new
البِيتُ بَعِيدٌ	The house is far
البَيْتَانِ بَعِيْدَانِ	The two houses are far
البُيُوتُ بَعِيْدَةٌ	The houses are far
السَّيَّارَةُ بَيْضَاءُ	The car is white.

The Doer الفَاعِلُ:

The word الفَاعِلُ in Arabic literally means "the doer", "the actor", "the worker", "labourer", "perpetrator", etc. As a grammatical term it refers to the active subject of a verbal clause. In other words, the noun denoting the doer of an action in a verbal sentence is referred to as الفَاعِلُ. When we speak of "the doer of the verb" we mean that noun representing the actor of the verb, or the agent involved in the act indicated by the verb. In Arabic for a noun to be classified as a doer it must always come after the verb and not before it. e.g.

Zaid is writing a letter.	يَكْتُبُ زَيْدٌ رِسَالَةً
Fatimah ate an apple.	أَكَلَتْ فَاطِمَةُ تُفَاحَةً
Ismail plucked a flower.	قَطَفَ إِسْمَاعِيلُ زَهْرَةً
Hamid is reading the Qur'an.	يَقْرَأُ حَامِدٌ القُرْآنَ
The mother opened the door.	فَتَحَتِ الأُمُّ البَابَ

Each of the underlined nouns in the above examples represents the doer of the verb, and we call such a noun الفَاعِلُ or the doer. The doer, as you can clearly see in the above Arabic sentences, is appearing after the verb. If this order is reversed and we start with a noun followed by a verb, it will no longer be the فَاعِلٌ (doer) in such a case but مُبْتَدَأ (subject). In other words, the sentence will be converted by such an action from a verbal sentence to a nominal sentence and the laws we discussed under المبتدأ (subject) and الخبر (predicate) will be applied. e.g.

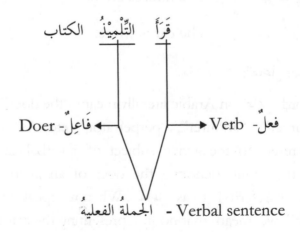

34

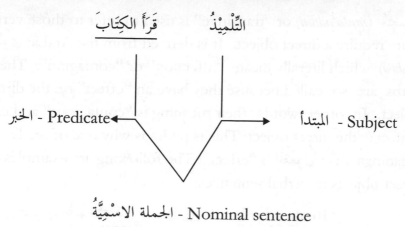

قَرَأَ الكِتَابَ التِّلْمِيْذُ

الخَبر - Predicate ←→ المُبْتَدأ - Subject

الجملة الاسْمِيَّةُ - Nominal sentence

Although the above two sentences differ in terms of grammatical construction, they convey the same meaning:

قَرَأَ التِّلْمِيْذُ الكِتَابَ   The student read the book.

التِّلْمِيْذُ قَرَأَ الكِتَابَ   The Student read the book.

The Direct Object المَفْعُولُ :

The word المَفْعُولُ (al-maf'ul) is derived from the verb فَعَل which means "to do", "to act", etc. In a verbal sentence the term المَفْعُولُ denotes the direct object or thing upon which the action of the doer occurs. Not all verbs is Arabic requires a direct object (المَفْعُولُ), others do not require a direct object. For example: جَلَسَ (he sat) in the sentence جَلَسَ حَامِدٌ (Hamid sat) does not require a direct object in order to complete the meaning of the sentence. However the verb أَكَل (He ate) in the sentence أَكَلَ زَيدٌ خُبْزاً (Zaid ate bread) needs a direct object, and in this case it is the word خُبْزاً "bread". Those verbs such as جَلَسَ that do not require a direct object to complete the meaning are called لَازِمٌ (laazim) or intransitive verbs. The word

مُتَعَـدٍّ (*muta'addin*) or "transitive" is used to refer to those verbs that require a direct object. It is derived from the Arabic عَدْوَى ('*adwa*) which literally means "infection" or "contagion". These verbs are so called because they have an "effect" on the direct object. In other words their meaning is "contagious" and can "infect" the direct object. This is perhaps why one of the literal meanings of المَفْعُولُ is "effect". The following are examples of direct objects in verbal sentences:

Ibrahim broke the <u>idols</u>.	كَسَرَ إِبْرَاهِيمُ الأَصْنَامَ
Muhammad helped <u>Amr</u>.	نَصَرَ مُحَمَّدٌ عَمْراً
Allah sent <u>Muhammad</u>.	أَرْسَلَ اللهُ مُحَمَّداً
Zainab drank the <u>water</u>.	شَرِبَتْ زَيْنَبُ المَاءَ
Bilal memorised the <u>Qur'an</u>.	حَفِظَ بِلاَلٌ القُرْآنَ

Each of the underlined words in the above examples is a direct object or المَفْعُولُ. In the first example, the action of "breaking" occurred on "the idols". All the verbs in the above sentences are transitive (مُتَعَـدٍّ) since they have an effect on the direct object.

SUMMARY

الجملة الاسمية = المبتدأ + الخبر

(subject + predicate = nominal sentence)

الجملة الفعلية = الفعل + الفاعل (المفعول)

(verb + doer or + direct object = verbal sentence)

36

IMPORTANT TERMS

1) المبتدأ   The Subject.

2) الخبر   The Predicate.

3) الفاعل   The Doer.

4) المفعول   The Direct object.

EXERCISE TWO

1- What is meant by the following terms; provide an example for each in a complete sentence.

المبتدأ   الخبر   الفاعل   المفعول

2- Construct sentences using the following words as subjects:

الدَّرْسُ   البَابُ   البَيْتُ   المَرْأَةُ   الرِّسَالةُ

3- Construct sentences using the following words and predicates:

عَلَى المَكْتَبِ   فِي المَسْجِدِ   يَقْرَأُ   جَمِيلٌ   قَائِمٌ

4- Identify the doer and the direct object in the following sentences:

1. أَكَلَتْ فَاطِمَةُ التُّفَاحَةَ   Fatima ate the apple

2. قَتَلَ دَاوُدُ جَالُوتَ   David killed Goliath

3. فَهِمَ التِّلْمِيذُ الدَّرْسَ   The student understood the lesson

4. شَرِبَ إِسْمَاعِيلُ اللَّبَنَ   Ismail drank the milk

5. رَأَى النَاسُ القَمَرَ   The people saw the moon

6. خَلَقَ اللهُ السَّمَاءَ   Allah created the sky

5 – Translate into English and analyse the grammatical construction of the following sentences. e.g.

1) زَيْدٌ قَائِمٌ   Zaid is standing

زَيْدٌ: مبتدأ

قَائِمٌ: خبر

المبتدأ و الخبر= الجملة الاسمية

2) قَرَأَ التِّلْمِيذُ الكِتَابَ   The student read the book

قَرَأَ: الفعل الماضى

التِّلْمِيذُ: فاعل

الكتابُ : مفعول

الفعل والفاعل = الجملة الفعلية.

١) خَلقَ اللهُ السَّمَاءَ .

٢) المسجدُ بعيدٌ .

٣) غَسَلَتْ البِنْتُ الثِّيَابَ .

٤) يَشرَبُ إسْمَاعِيلُ مَاءاً.

٥) الوَلَدُ يَغْسِلُ السَّيَّارَةَ.

٦) الأُمُّ فِي الجَامِعَةِ .

Chapter Three

الإعْرَابُ والبناءُ

المَرْفُوعُ والمَنْصُوبُ والمَجْرُورُ والمَجْزُومُ والمَبْنِيُّ

Declension and Indeclension

Arabic words have signs written above or below each letter helping the speaker to pronounce the letters. These signs are referred to as the الحَرَكَاتُ (*al-harakat*) or vowels.

There are three basic vowels or حَرَكَاتٌ :

a) الضَّمَّةُ, *Dammah* (vowel u), which is indicated by the stroke ——— drawn over the letter e.g.

بُ "bu"

b) الفَتْحَةُ , *Fathah* (vowel a), which is indicated by the stroke ——— drawn over the letter e.g.

بَ "ba"

c) الكَسْرَةُ , *Kasrah* (vowel i), which is indicated by the stroke ——— drawn under the letter e.g.

بِ "bi"

Apart from *dammah, fathah* , and *kasrah*, there are two other signs:

a) السُّكُون , *Al-sukun* (Anti- vowel). The absence of a vowel is indicated by a small circle drawn over the letter e.g.

بْ

b) التَّشْدِيــدُ, *Al-tashdid.* If there is a double letter in a word where the first letter has no vowel (it has a *sukun*) then followed by a *vowelled* letter, the letter is not written twice, instead a *tashdid* (ﹼ) is written over the letter indicating that the letter is duplicated e.g.

مَرَّ - Which means "he passed by", was originally مَرَرَ

سَبَّ –Which means "he insulted", was originally سَبَبَ

The vowel of the last letter of the word signifies the *end-case* of the word; it changes according to the grammatical function of the word e.g.

The professor came. جَاءَ الأُسْتَاذُ

The word الأُسْتَاذُ (professor) has the vowel ضَمَّةٌ (ُ) as its end-case since grammatically it is the فَاعِلٌ (doer) of the verb جَاءَ (he came).

I saw the professor. رَأَيْتُ الأُسْتَاذَ

Here the word الأُسْتَاذ has the vowel فَتْحَةٌ (َ) as its end-case since grammatically it is the مَفْعُولٌ (direct object) of رَأَيْتُ (I saw).

I passed by the professor. مَرَرْتُ بالأُسْتَاذ

The word الأُسْتَاذ has the vowel كَسْرَةٌ as its end-case since it is preceded by the particle بِ (by) which is a preposition.

In Arabic a word may have any of these signs as its *end-case,* which will change according to its grammatical function, or position in the sentence, from one *end-case* to another, this change is called الإعْــرَابُ or declension. The word, which undergoes such a change, is called المُعْرَبُ or the declinable word.

Some Arabic words maintain one vowel on or below their last letter which will not change, such words are the opposite of the declinable or المُعْرَبُ and are called المَبْنِيُّ or the indeclinable word. This inability to change the vowels at the ending of a word is called البِنَاءُ (indeclinability) e.g.

These people came.	جَاءَ هؤُلاءِ
I saw these people.	رَأَيْتُ هؤُلاءِ
I passed by these people.	مَرَرْتُ بِهؤُلاءِ

From the above examples you will notice that the word هؤُلاءِ refuses to change its end-case in three different grammatical situations, and it has the same vowel in all the cases. The following are examples of some of the words that refuse to change their end-case vowels:

أَيْنَ   حَيْثُ   مُنْذُ   أَمْسِ   حَذَامِ   مَنْ   كَمْ

هَذِهِ   هَذَا   كَيْفَ

However, the majority of nouns in Arabic are مُعْـــرَبٌ or declinable. Amongst the three types of verbs only the مُضَارِع (present tense) is مُعْـــرَبٌ . The مَـــاضٍ (past tense) and أَمْرٌ (imperative) are مَبْنِيٌّ (indeclinable). All the حُرُوف or particles are مَبْنِيٌّ .

There are four end-cases for the declinable word - المُعْرَبُ :

a) المَرْفُـــوعُ -*The Nominative:* The nominative is a word which has a ضَمَّةٌ as its end-case (or the representatives of ضَمَّةٌ

which will be discussed later). The nominative case ending or الرَّفْعُ applies to the noun and the present tense verb e.g.

يَذْهَبُ زَيْدٌ إِلَى السُّوقِ   Zaid in going to the market

زَيْدٌ يَذْهَبُ إِلَى المَسْجِدِ   Zaid is going to the Mosque

In the above examples the verb يَذْهَبُ and the noun زَيْدٌ are in the nominative form since they both have ضَمَّةٌ as their end-case.

b) المَنْصُوبُ *The Accusative*: The accusative is the word having a فَتْحَـةٌ or its representatives as the end-case. The accusative case ending or النَّصْبُ applies to the noun and the verb e.g.

لَنْ يَذْهَبَ زَيْدٌ إِلَى الهِنْد   Zaid will never go to India

رَأَيْتُ زَيْداً   I saw Zaid.

c) المَجْرُورُ *The Genitive*: The genitive is the word having a كَسْرَةٌ as the end case. The genitive case ending or الجَرُّ applies to the noun only e.g.

الكِتَابُ عَلَى المَكْتَبِ   The book is on the desk

رَسُولُ اللهِ   The Prophet of God

d) المَجْزُومُ *The Jussive*: The jussive is the word having a سُكُونٌ as the end case. The jussive case ending or الجَزْمُ applies to the verb only e.g.

لَا تَذْهَبْ   Don't go!

لَمْ يَذْهَبْ   He didn't go

The noun will assume the nominative case when it is one of the following categories:

1. The subject of a nominal sentence (المُبْتَدأ) e.g.

    الرَّجُلُ طَويلٌ   The man is tall.

2. The predicate of a nominal sentence (الخبر) e.g.

    اَلْمَاءُ حَارٌّ   The water is hot.

3. The doer (فَاعِلٌ) of a verb in a verbal sentence e.g.

    إجْتَهَدَ حَامِدٌ   Hamid worked hard.

4. The substitute of the doer (نَائِبُ الفَاعِلِ) in a verbal sentence e.g

    ضُرِبَ زَيْدٌ   Zaid was hit.

The noun will assume the accusative end-case in the following instance:

المَفْعُولُ - The direct object in a verbal sentence e.g.

أكَلَ زَيْدٌ طَعَاماً   Zaid ate food.

The noun will assume the genitive end-case in the following instance:

When it occurs after a preposition or حَرْفُ الجَرِّ e.g.

عَلِيٌّ مِنَ المَدِيْنَةِ   Ali is from Madina

NOTE: There are more instances when the noun will assume the nominative, accusative and genitive end-cases. These will be discussed at a later point.

The verb will assume the nominative end case when it is not preceded by any of the *subjunctive particles* or الحُرُوفُ النَّاصِبَة , nor by any of the *jussive particles* or حُرُوفُ الجَزْمِ e.g.

المضارع المَجْزوم	المضارع المنصوب	المضارع المرفوع
لَمْ يَذْهَبْ	أَنْ يَذْهَبَ	يَذْهَبُ
لَمَا يَكْتُبْ	لَنْ يَكْتُبَ	يَكْتُبُ
لِيَنْصُرْ	كَي يَنْصُرَ	يَنْصُرُ
لا تَضْرِبْ	إذَن يَضْرِبَ	يَضْرِبُ
إنْ يَجْتَهِدْ	--------------	يَجْتَهِدُ

The categories of Indeclinable words (المَبْنيّ) will be discussed later. They include some nouns, the past and imperative verbs and all the particles e.g.

نَحْنُ الطُّلَابُ . (مَبْنيٌّ عَلَى الضَّمَةِ)   <u>We</u> are students.

كَيْفَ حَالُكَ ؟ (مَبْنيٌّ عَلَى الفَتْحَةِ)   <u>How</u> are you?

هذِه جَامِعَةٌ . (مَبْنيٌّ عَلَى الكَسْرَة)   <u>This is </u>a university.

هذَا بَيْتٌ . (مَبْنيٌّ عَلَى السُّكُونِ)   <u>The is </u>a house.

SUMMARY

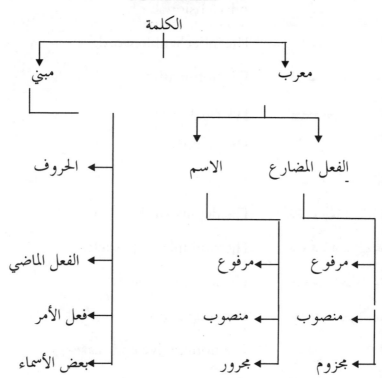

IMPORTANT TERMS

1-	الحركات	*Al-harakat* The vowels.
2-	الضمة	*Al-dammah* (vowel u)
3-	الفتحة	*Al-fathah* (vowel a)
4-	الكسرة	*Al-kasrah* (vowel i)
5-	السكون	*Al-sukun* (anti- vowel)
6-	التشديد	*Al-tashdid*
7-	الاعراب	Declension

45

8-	المعرب	The declinable word.
9-	البناء	Indeclension
10-	المبني	The indeclianble word.
11-	المرفوع	The nominative
12-	المنصوب	The accusative
13-	المجرور	The genitive
14-	المجزوم	The jussive
15-	نائب الفاعل	The deputy of the doer
16-	حروف النصب	The subjunctive particles
17-	حروف الجزم	The jussive particles
18-	حروف الجرّ	The prepositions
19-	الرفع	The nominative end- case
20-	النصب	The accusative end- case
21-	الجرّ	The genitive end- case
22-	الجزم	The jussive end-case

EXERCISE THREE

What is meant by the following terms. Give an example for each one in a complete sentence.

a) المعرب	b) المبني	c) المرفوع
d) المنصوب	e) المجرور	f) المجزوم

1. Analyse the end-case of the underlined words e.g.

كَتَبَ مُحَمَّدٌ الرِّسَالَةَ

كَتَبَ = الفعل الماضي، مبنيٌّ عَلَى الفَتْحَة

محمدٌ = فاعلٌ، مَرْفُوعٌ بالضَّمَّةِ

الرِّسَالَةَ = مَفْعُولٌ، مَنْصُوبٌ بالفَتْحَةِ

i)	This is a mosque	هذا مسجدٌ
ii)	The teacher is in the class	المُدَرِّسُ في الفَصْلِ
iii)	Hamid read the lesson	قَرَأَ حَامِدٌ الدَّرْسَ
iv)	The chair is broken	الكُرسِيُّ مَكْسُورٌ
v)	Zaid hit Amr	ضَرَبَ زَيْدٌ عَمْراً
vi)	The Professor is going to the class	يَذْهَبُ الأُسْتَاذُ إِلَى الفَصْلِ

3) Translate and vocalise the following sentences:

a) لم يرجع حسن من السوق

b) هذه حديقة

b) خلق الله الأرض

c) الرجل ينصر الفقير

d) حفظ إبراهيم القُرآن

e) أكل محمد خبزا

f) لم يضرب زيد الكلب

g) لن ينصر الله الظالم

h) الطعام لذيذ

i) الصورة جميلة

4) Translate the following into English:

عَنْ ابْنِ عُمَرَ رضي الله عنْهُمَا قَالَ: قَالَ رَسُولُ اللّهِ صَلَّــى اللهُ عليــهِ وَآلِــهِ وَسَلَّم: بُنِيَ الإسْلاَمُ عَلَى خَمْسٍ: شَهَادَة أَنْ لا إلَهَ إلاَّ اللّهُ وَأَنَّ مُحَمَّداً رَسُولُ اللّهِ، و إقَامِ الصَّلاةِ، وَإِيتَاءِ الزَّكَاةِ، والْحَجِّ، وصَوْمِ رَمَضَان –رواه البخاري

Chapter Four

المَعْرِفَةُ و النَّكَرَةُ

The Definite and Indefinite Noun

During our discussion on the characteristics of a noun in chapter one, we briefly introduced the concept of *the definite noun*. We also mentioned that this topic would be discussed in detail in chapter four. In this chapter we will look at all other forms of the definite noun. In Arabic a noun is either *definite* مَعْرِفَةٌ (*ma'rifah*) or *indefinite* نَكِرَةٌ (*nakrah*). When a noun is used to refer to an unspecified or undefined person or thing, it is called الاسْمُ النَّكِرَةُ or the indefinite noun e.g.

كِتَابٌ   <u>a</u> book (any book)

رَجُلٌ   <u>a</u> man (any man)

تُفَّاحٌ   <u>an</u> apple (any apple)

The indefinite noun النَّكَرَةُ - - generally has the *tanwin,* and is translated in English as "a" or "an". The تَنْوِينٌ or nunation is an *unvowelled* and *unwritten* ن (*nun*) at the end of a noun and is indicated by the duplication of the final vowel in the word and appears as double vowels ⸺ on the last letter in a word. For example:

كِتَابًا – كِتَابٍ كِتَابْنْ كِتَابٌ – كِتَابْنْ – كِتَابْنْ

In cases where a nunnated word is in the accusative form, indicated by double *fathah,* the letter *alif* (١) is added. But if the word ends with the letter (ة) التَاءُ المَرْبُوْطَة - (*al-taa' al-marbutah*) - the letter *alif* will not be added e.g.

بَيْتاً – مَدِينَةً – شَمْساً – خَلِيْفَةً – جِدَارَةً – مَدَرَسَةً – بِنْتاً

When a noun is used to denote a specific person, place, or thing, it is called الاسْمُ المَعْرِفَة or the definite noun. In Arabic there is no equivalent for the English "the", therefore, another way of making a noun definite is to prefix it with the *definite article* (ال) which is referred to in Arabic as (أَدَاةُ التَّعْرِيْفِ). When this definite article has been prefixed the noun automatically loses its nunation or *tanwin* e.g

الكِتَابُ = أل + كِتَابٌ   The book.

البَيتُ = أل + بيتٌ   The house.

It will be wrong to say الكِتَابٌ or البَيْتٌ with nunation.

The particle أل which we said is called أَدَاةُ التَّعْرِيْفِ or the definite article is generally translated as "the" in English. When it is prefixed to the indefinite noun (الاسْمُ النَّكِرَةُ) it converts it into a definite noun (الاسْــمُ المَعْرِفــةُ). When a noun has been converted into a definite noun, it qualifies to be a subject (المُبْتَدَأُ) of a nominal sentence (الجُمْلَةُ الاسْمِيَّةُ), since an indefinite noun cannot be a subject. The predicate, however, must be indefinite, as we have already seen in chapter two, e.g.

الدَّرْسُ وَاضِحٌ   The lesson is clear.

اللَّيْلُ مُظْلِمٌ   The night is dark.

الكِتَابُ مُفِيْدٌ   The book is useful.

The noun made definite in this way is called المُعَرَّفَةُ باللاَّم. Apart from this noun there are six other nouns which are also classified as definite nouns, these are:

1) الضَّمِيرُ - The personal pronoun: The personal pronouns are words which refer to the speaker, the second and third persons e.g.

نَحْنُ   هُوَ   هِي   أَنْتِ   أَنْتَ   أَنَا

2) إِسْمُ الإِشَارَة - The demonstrative pronoun: The demonstrative pronouns are the words used to demonstrate or point out some object or person e.g.

هَؤُلاَءِ   هَتَان   هَذَان   هَذِهِ   هَذَا

أُولآئِكَ   تَانِكَ   ذَانِكَ   تِلْكَ   ذَلِكَ

3) إِسْمُ المَوْصُول - The relative pronoun: The relative pronouns are words which have a connection or relation to the sentence mentioned after them e.g.

اللاَتِي   الَّذِينَ   اللَّتَان   الَّتِي   الَّذِي

4) المُضَافُ إِلى مَعْرِفَةٍ - The noun annexed to any definite noun e.g.

كِتَابُ اللهِ – بَابُ البَيْتِ – دِيْنُنَا – رَبُّ هَذَا البَيْتِ

5) المُنَادَى - The noun of the vocative: The noun of the vocative refers to the noun that follows the حَرْفُ النِّدَاء or vocative particle e.g.

يَا + زَيْدٌ = يَا زَيْدُ   O Zaid!

51

The يَـا (*yaa*) in the beginning of the name Zaid is the *vocative particle* (حَرْفُ النِّدَاءِ), and the name Zaid is the *noun of the vocative* (الْمُنَـادَى). The following are examples of some of the vocative particles used in Arabic:

O Zaid, approach	أ = أَزَيْدُ أَقْبِلْ!
O Ibrahim, sit down	أَيْ = أَيْ إِبْرَاهِيْمُ اجْلِسْ!
O Muhammad, come	هَيَا = مُحَمَّدُ تَعَالَ!

When using the vocative particle يَا before a noun, one must make sure that the noun is not prefixed with the definitive particle ال e.g.

يَا رَجُلُ	O man!
يَا بِنْتُ	O girl!
يَا وَلَدُ	O boy!

However, if the noun of the vocative is prefixed with the definite particle ال, the following vocative particles must be put between the vocative noun (الْمُنَادَى) and the vocative particle (حَرْفُ النِّدَاءِ):

(a) أَيُّهَا (for a masculine vocative noun) e.g.

يَا أَيُّهَا النَّبِيُّ حَسْبُكَ اللهُ وَمَنِ اتَّبَعَكَ مِنَ الْمُؤْمِنِيْنَ

"O Apostle! God is sufficient for you and those who follow you from among the believers..."

(b) أَيَّتُهَا (for a feminine vocative noun) e.g.

يَا أَيَّتُهَا النَّفْسُ الْمُطْمَئِنَّةُ   *"O you contented soul!..."*

The above two Qur'anic verses given as example are written in the Qur'an as follows: يَأَيُّهَا and يَأَيَّتُهَا. This has to do with the style Qur'anic script (*rasm al-qur'an*) and does not affect the grammar laws we are discussing.

When the vocative noun is العَلَمُ المُفْرَدُ (simple proper noun) it will be indeclinable (مَبْنِيٌّ). In this case the indeclinability is indicated by a single الضَّمَة (——) on the last letter. However, if the vocative particle is followed by العَلَمُ المُرَكَّبُ (composited proper noun), the noun will be put in the accusative form. A *simple proper noun* is a proper noun that is in the form of a single word e.g.

مُحَمَّدٌ (يَا مُحَمَّدُ)   زَيْدٌ (يَا زَيْدُ)   خَدِيْجَةٌ (يَا خَدِيْجَةُ)

The composited proper noun is the proper noun that is made up of two or more words e.g.

عَبْدُ الله (يَا عَبْدَ الله) عَبْدُ الرَّحْمن (يَا عَبْدَ الرَّحْمن) أَمَةُ الله (يَا أَمَةَ الله) إِبْنُ أُمِّي (يَا ابْنَ أُمِّي) عَبْدُ رَبِّ الكَعْبَةِ (يَا عَبْدَ رَبِّ الكَعْبَةِ) مَعْشَرُ الشَّبَاب (يَــــا مَعْشَرَ الشَّبَاب)

The noun of the vocative is treated as المَفْعُولُ (direct object). When one says (يَا زَيْدُ) it is understood that he is saying (أَدْعُو زَيْدًا) or "I am calling Zaid!" The action of calling is occurring on Zaid. The verb أَدْعُو has been deleted and replaced with the vocative particle يَــا as a shortened form of the long أَدْعُو زَيْدًا. The following is how vocative particle and vocative noun are analysed:

O boy!   يَا وَلَدُ

يا : حَرْفُ النِّدَاء مَبْنِيٌّ على السُّكُون

ولد : مُنَادَى مَبْنِيٌّ على الضَّمَّةِ فِي مَحَلِّ النَّصْبِ (مَفْعُولٌ بِهِ)

يا عبدَ الله   O Abdallah!

يا : حَرْفُ النداءِ مَبنيٌّ على السُّكُون

عبد : مُنَادَى مَنْصُوبٌ وَ مُضَافٌ

الله : لَفْظُ الجَلَالَةِ، مَجْرُورٌ ، مُضَافٌ إليهِ

6) إِسْمُ العَلَم - The proper noun: A proper name in Arabic is referred to as (إِسْمُ العَلَم). Proper names are usually names of people or places. They are always definite and generally not prefixed with أل, the *tanwin* in such a case is not translated e.g.

مُحَمَّدٌ	Muhammad (name of a particular person)
زَيْدٌ	Zaid (name of a particular person)
خَدِيْجَةٌ	Khadijah (name of a particular place)
جدَّةٌ	Jeddah (name of a city in Saudi Arabia)

However, some proper names may be prefixed with the particle ال and this usually happens in the names of places e.g.

القَاهِرَةُ	Cairo
العِرَاقُ	Iraq
الإِسْكَنْدَرِيَّةُ	Alexandria (city in Northern Egypt)

When definite particle appears before a noun commencing with any of the *Sun letters* (الحُرُوفُ الشَّمْسِيَّةُ), it will not be pronounced, instead it is assimilated into the sun letter e.g.

ش: الشَّجَرَةُ	ت: التِّجَارَةُ
ص: الصِّرَاطُ	ث: الثَّمَرَةُ
ض: الضِّفْدَعُ	د: الدَّرْسُ

ط: الطَّاهِرُ	ذ: الذِّكْرُ
ظ: الظَّالِمُ	ر: الرَّسُولُ
ل: اللَّيْمُون	ز: الزَّوجُ
ن: النِّسَاءُ	س: السَّجَادَةُ

The opposite applies to the *Moon letters* (الْحُرُوفُ الْقَمَرِيَّةُ), the أل in words commencing with these letters is pronounced e.g.

ف: الفِيلُ	أ: الأُسْرةُ
ق: القَاهِرةُ	ب: البَيْتُ
ك: الكَعْبَةُ	ج: الجَبَلُ
م: المُهَنْدِسُ	ح: الحَمْدُ
و: الوَيْلُ	خ: الخُبْزُ
ها: الهِجْرَةُ	ع: العِبَادَةُ
ي: اليومُ	غ: الغَضَبُ

The letter *alif* (ا) is actually neither a sun nor moon letter since it is never the first letter of a word and is always vowel less - ساكن e.g.

طَعَامٌ   كِتَابٌ   جِدَارٌ

The *hamzah* (ء) , however, is a moon letter and appears as the first letter in some words. It can appear as vowelled مُتَحَرِّكٌ or unvowelled سَاكِنٌ e.g.

أَكَلَ   أُنْصُرْ   إِنْسَانٌ   -   فَأْسٌ   بِئْرٌ   سَمَاءٌ

The *initial hamzah* (*hamzah* appearing as the first letter of a word) will be one of two:

a) هَمْزَةُ القَطْعِ (*hamzat al-qat'i*) The separative *hamzah*

b) هَمْزَةُ الوَصْلِ (*hamzat al-wasli*) The connective *hamzah*

The separative *hamzah* هَمْزَةُ القَطْعِ is always pronounced, and is written above or below the *alif* e.g.

إِبْلٌ   أَمْرٌ   أُخْتٌ

NOTE: The sign ء is actually the *hamzah*. The letter *alif* serves only as a seat for the *hamzah*. At times the letter و and letter ي may also serve as a seat for the *hamzah* (ء), and sometimes the *hamzah* is used without a seat e.g.

قِرَاءَةٌ   –   قُرِئَ   -   جَاؤُوا

The connective *hamzah* (همزة الوصل) is only written and pronounced at the beginning of a sentence, in other cases it is neither written nor pronounced e.g.

أُكْتُبْ يَا وَلَدُ ، يَا وَلَدُ اكْتُبْ

الكِتَابُ جَدِيدٌ ، إِفْتَحِ الكِتَابَ

The connective *hamzah* occurs in the definite article ال in some nouns such as:

إِبْنٌ   إِبْنَةٌ   إِسْمٌ   إِمْرَأَةٌ   إِثْنَانِ   إِثْنَتَانِ   إِمْرُؤٌ

And also in certain verb forms and their *verbal nouns* e.g.

أُكْتُبْ   إِجْلِسْ   إِنْكَسَرَ   إِجْتَهَدَ   إِسْتَغْفَرَ

إِنْكِسَارٌ   إِجْتِهَادٌ   إِسْتِغْفَارٌ

Out of the seven categories of الاسْمُ المعرفةُ discussed above, three are declinable and the rest are indeclinable:

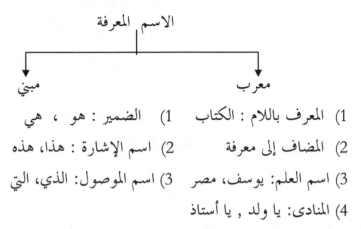

الاسم المعرفة

مبني   معرب

مبني	معرب
1) المعرف باللام : الكتاب	1) الضمير : هو ، هي
2) المضاف إلى معرفة	2) اسم الإشارة : هذا، هذه
3) اسم العلم: يوسف، مصر	3) اسم الموصول: الذي، التي
	4) المنادى: يا ولد , يا أستاذ

IMPORTANT TERMS

1. الاسم النكرة   The indefinite noun

2. الاسم المعرفة   The definite noun

3. أداة التعريف   The definite article

4. الضمير   The personal pronoun

5. الاسم الإشارة   The demonstrative pronoun

6. إسم الموصول   The relative pronoun

7. المضاف إلى معرفة   The noun annexed to any definite noun

8. المنادى   The noun of the vocative

9. حرف النداء   The vocative particle

10. إسم العلم   The proper noun

11. الحروف الشمسية   The sun letters

12. الحروف القمرية   The moon letters

13. همزة القطع   The seperative *hamzah*

14. همزة الوصل   The connective *hamzah*

15. العلم المركب   The composited proper noun

16. العلم المفرد   The simple proper noun

EXERCISE EIGHT

1 - State which of the following nouns are معرفة and which are نكرة and if the former, mention which type:

قَلَنْسُوة   هذه   الرسول   خديجة   امرأة   مدرستنا

جيشٌ   التي   يا بنات   خاتم   أولائك   إسمي

أنت   أُرْدُن   الجاهد   مسجد النبي   مريم

الذين   قلم زيد   الأنبياء

2 – Translate the following into Arabic :

   i)   Ibrahim is from Jordan and his wife is from Afghanistan

   ii)   These women are student at the university

   iii)   Our Professor (fem) is hard working

   iv)   O Muhammad! Go to the market.

   v)   The colour of this car is beautiful.

   vi)   The author of this book is a teacher

   vii)   Zaid's book is old and Fatima's book is new

   viii)   My house is near and your house is far

   ix)   This is a clever and strong woman

3 – Translate the following into English:

عَنْ جَابِرٍ رَضِيَ اللّه عَنْهُ قَالَ: قال رَسُولُ اللّه صَلَّى اللّه عليهِ وآله وَسَــــلَّمَ: لا تَأْكُلُوا بِالشِّمَال فَإِنَّ الشَّيْطَانَ يَأْكُلُ بِالشِّمَال. رواه مسلم

4 - Prefix the definite article to each of the following words:

شَارِعٌ – مَلِكٌ – امرَأَةٌ – قَصْرٌ – إِنْسَانٌ – لَحْمٌ – صَادِقٌ – وَاسِعٌ – حِمَارٌ – خَيَّاطٌ

5 - Translate the following sentences into English:

الرَّبِيعُ جَمِيلٌ	القِصَّةُ عَجِيبَةٌ	السَّمَاءُ صَافِيَةٌ
الشَّمْسُ مُشْرِقَةٌ	السَّاعَةُ جَدِيْدَةٌ	الشَّارِعُ وَاسِعٌ
العَذَابُ شَدِيْدٌ	التَّمْرُ حُلْوٌ	مُحَمَّدٌ رَسُوْلٌ

6 - Translate the following into Arabic:

a) An apple   b) The donkey.   c) A river

d) A woman   e) The street   f) A mountain

g) The doctor.   h) A horse.   i) The farmer.

j) A teacher

Chapter Five

الجِنْسُ: المُذَكَّرُ و المُؤَنَّثُ

Gender: The Masculine And Feminine Noun

Arabic is a gender specific language and nouns as well as verbs are classified in gender terms. In Arabic a noun has two genders, masculine or مُذَكَّرٌ and feminine (مُؤَنَّثٌ) According to Abdullah bin Aqil (698-769 A.H.), the famous commentator of the groundbreaking grammar poem, the *al-Fiyah* of Jamal al-Din Ibn Malik (600-672 A.H., "all nouns are originally masculine and the feminine is a derivative from the masculine. Since the masculine is the origin, it requires no special characteristics that shows its masculinity. However, since the feminine is a derivative from the masculine, it requires certain distinguishing features that denote its femininity..."[2]

Controversial as it may sound from a contemporary sociolinguistic point of view, this is how classical Arabic grammarians viewed language. There is no special sign for identifying masculine words, and words should be assumed to be masculine unless they belong to one of the following categories:

---

[2] *Sharh Ibn Aqil,* Tehran: Ahmadi Publishers, 1980, vol. 2, p.111.

a) Words feminine by meaning, المُؤَنَّثُ الحَقِيقِيُّ (female human beings or animals). Scholars explain this kind of مُؤَنَّث as that feminine which has its male opposite e.g.

أُمٌّ	-	mother	بِنْتٌ	-	girl	عَرُوسٌ	- bride
إِمْرَأَةٌ	-	woman	أُخْتٌ	-	sister	زَوْجَةٌ	- wife
لَبُؤَةٌ	-	lioness	بَقَرَةٌ	-	cow	دَجَاجَةٌ	- hen

There are also words which do not necessarily have a male opposite and yet they are classified as المُؤَنَّثُ الحَقِيقِيُّ because their meaning is only true in the female gender e.g.

حَامِلٌ   Pregnant

مُرْضِعٌ   Wet nurse

حَائِضٌ   a menstruating lady

b) Conventional feminine (مُؤَنَّثٌ حُكْمِيٌّ), indicating nouns of things not truly feminine but follow a conventional rule. It includes the following :

1) Nouns ending with التَّاءُ المَرْبُوطَةُ or letter ة also known as the round *taa'*. The letter ة is considered as the basic feminine sign e.g.

| شَجَرَةٌ - tree | مَدْرَسَةٌ - school | مَدِينَةٌ - city |
| أُمَّةٌ - nation | نَافِذَةٌ - window | سَيَّارَةٌ - car |

The ة is also added to masculine nouns or adjectives to make them feminine e.g.

مَلِكٌ – مَلِكَةٌ – خَادِمٌ – خَادِمَةٌ – إِبْنٌ – إِبْنَةٌ

كَبِيرٌ – كَبِيرَةٌ – جَمِيلٌ – جَمِيلَةٌ – جَدِيدٌ – جَدِيدَةٌ

If however the noun ending with ة clearly indicates a male it will be masculine e.g.

طَلْحَةٌ - Talha (name of a person)   خَلِيْفَةٌ - caliph

2) Nouns ending with the shortened *alif* الأَلِفُ المَقْصُورَةُ (*al-alif al-maqsurah*) e.g.

سَلْمَى بُشْرَى ظَمْأَى مُسْتَشْفَى حَلْوَى لَيْلَى سَلْوَى

3) Nouns ending with the elongated *alif* الأَلِفُ المَمْدُودَةُ (*al-alif al-mamdudah*) e.g.

هَيْفَاءُ –حَمْرَاءُ –حَسْنَاءُ – بَيْدَاءُ – عُلْيَاءُ – صَحْرَاءُ – كِبْرِيَاءُ –صَفْرَاءُ

The above three categories are assumed to be feminine since they have a feminine sign, namely:

The ة of feminisation, the shortened *alif*, and the elongated *alif*. However some nouns are feminine without having a feminine ending. The following are categories of such nouns without a feminine sign:

a) Names of towns, cities and countries are feminine e.g.

دِمَشْق - Damascus   بَغْدَاد - Baghdad   يَمَن - Yemen

b) All parts of the body which are in pairs e.g.

عَيْنٌ - Eye   أُذْنٌ - ear   يَدٌ -hand   رِجْلٌ – leg

c) Names of females with no feminine sign e.g.

زَيْنَبُ   مَرَيَمُ   سُعَادُ   هِنْدُ   كُلْثُومُ

d) Nouns feminine by common usage مُؤَنَّث سَمَاعِي e.g.

أَرْضٌ-earth   نَفْسٌ - soul   رِيحٌ - wind   دَارٌ - house

شَمْسٌ -sun   بِئْرٌ - well   حَرْبٌ - war   نَارٌ - fire

SUMMARY

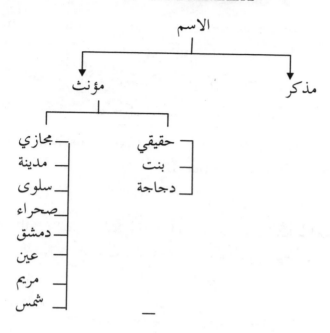

IMPORTANT TERMS

1) المذكر   The masculine noun.

2) المؤنث   The feminine noun.

3) مؤنث حقيقي Real feminine (feminine by meaning)

4) مؤنث حكمي Conventional feminine

5) التاء المربوطة *At-ta al- marbutah* (The basic sign of feminine)

6) الألف المقصورة The shortened *alif.*

7) الألف الممدودة The elongated *alif.*

8) المؤنث السماعي Nouns feminine by common usage.

EXERCISE FIVE

1) Translate the following sentences and then identify the gender of the underlined nouns, giving reasons:

اليَدُ نَظِيفَةٌ - الأُسْرَةُ كَبِيرَةٌ - لَيْلَى مُجْتَهِدَةٌ -
الأُمُّ رَحِيمَةٌ - الصَّحْرَاءُ وَاسِعَةٌ - الشَّمْسُ مُشْرِقَةٌ

2) Make full sentences, each consisting of two nouns, one from group A and another from group B:

A

المَاءُ ، النَّارُ ، السَّبُورَةُ ، الدَّارُ ، اللَّحْمُ ، الشَّحْمُ الفَحْمُ ، الذَّهْبُ ، الفِضَّةُ ، العُشْبُ ، التُّفَّاحَةُ ، الشَّجَرَةُ ، البَحْرُ ، البَقَرَةُ ، النَّهْرُ

B

وَاسِعَةٌ ، حَارَّةٌ ، عَذْبٌ ، مَلِحٌ ، سَائِلٌ ، أَبْيَضُ (بَيْضَاءُ) ، أَسْوَدُ (سَوْدَاءُ) ، أَحْمَرُ (حَمْرَاءُ) ، أَصْفَرُ (صَفْرَاءُ)، أَخْضَرُ (خَضْرَاءُ)

3) Translate the following into English:

قال رسول الله صلى الله عليه وآله وسلم: ثلاثة لا تُرَدُّ دَعْوَتُهم:الصائم حــتى يفطر ، والإمام العادل ودعوة المظلوم، يرفعها الله فوق الغمام، وتفتح لها أبواب السماء ، ويقول الرب : وعزتي وجلالي لأنصرنك ولو بعد حين.

64

Chapter Six

العَدَدُ : المُفْرَدُ و المُثَنَّى و الجَمْعُ

Number: The Singular, Dual And Plural

Nouns in Arabic are either singular (اَلْمُفْرَد) , dual (اَلْمُثَنَّى), or plural (اَلْجَمْعُ). The noun indicating one unit is called اَلْمُفْرَد, e.g.

A student (fem.) طَالِبَةٌ   A student (masc.) طَالِبٌ

A queen مَلِكَةٌ   A king مَلِكٌ

The noun indicating two units of the singular is called اَلْمُثَنَّى, the dual e.g.

Two students (fem.) طَالِبَتَان

two students (masc.) طَالِبَان

Two queens مَلِكَتَان

two kings مَلِكَان

The dual is formed by adding the letters *alif* + *nun* (ا + ن) when the noun is nominative مَرْفُوعٌ and the letters *yaa* + *nun* يْنِ preceded by a letter with a *fatha* (ـَـ) when the noun is accusative and genitive مَنْصُوبٌ / مَجْرُورٌ e.g.

مَرْفُوعٌ Nominative -	مَنْصُوبٌ Accusative -	مَجْرُورٌ Genitive -
جَاءَ الطَّالِبَان	رَأَيْتُ الطَّالِبَيْنِ	مَرَرْتُ بِالطَّالِبَيْنِ
الرَّجلَان طَوِيْلَان	نَصَرَ حَامِدٌ الرَّجلَيْنِ	ذَهَبْتُ إِلَى الرَّجلَيْنِ
البِنْتَان مُجْتَهِدَتَان	سَأَلَ الأُسْتَاذُ البِنْتَيْنِ	ذَهَبَتْ مَرْيَمُ مَعَ البِنْتَيْنِ
الكِتَابَان قَدِيْمَان	إِشْتَرَيْتُ الكِتَابَيْنِ	كَتَبْتُ فِى الكِتَابَيْنِ

The noun indicating three or more units is called (plural)الجمع e.g.

Singular - المُفرَدُ	Dual - المُثَنَّى	Plural - الجَمعُ
وَلَدٌ	وَلَدَان	أَولَادٌ
مُسْلِمٌ	مُسْلِمَان	مُسْلِمُونَ
مُسْلِمَةٌ	مُسْلِمَتَان	مُسْلِمَات
قَلَمٌ	قَلَمَان	أَقْلَامٌ
كَلْبٌ	كَلْبَان	كِلاَبٌ
بِنْتٌ	بِنْتَان	بَنَاتٌ
مَدرَسَةٌ	مَدَرَسَتَان	مَدَارِسٌ

There are two types of plural in Arabic:

a) الجَمْعُ السَّالِمُ   The sound plural.

b) الجَمْعُ المُكَسَّرُ   The broken plural.

The sound plural is formed from the singular by suffixing additional letters to it, it is called the sound plural because all the vowels and letters of the singular form are retained in it .i.e. the structure of its singular remains unchanged. The sound plural is further divided into two categories:

2- جَمْع مُذَكَّر سَالِم   The sound masculine plural

2- جَمْع مُؤَنَّث سَالِم   The sound feminine plural.

The sound masculine plural is a noun indicating three or more male objects. The singular maintains its structure, and the suffix ونَ is added in the case of nominative, and the suffix يْن

66

preceded by a letter with a *kasrah*, in the case of the accusative and genitive e.g.

المَرْفُوعُ Nominative	المَنْصُوبُ Accusative	المَجْرُورُ Genitive
جَاءَ المُسْلِمُونَ	رَأَيْتُ المُسْلِمِينَ	سَلَّمْتُ عَلَى المُسْلِمِينَ
المُؤْمِنُونَ صَائِمُونَ	خَاطَبَ اللهُ المُؤْمِنِينَ	مِنَ المُؤْمِنِينَ رِجَالٌ صَدَقُوا...
حَضَرَ المُعَلِّمُونَ	سَأَلَ الطُّلَّابُ المُعَلِّمِينَ	هَذِهِ كُتُبُ المُعَلِّمِينَ
المُهَنْدِسُونَ مُجْتَهِدُونَ	اسْتَأْجَرَ المَصْنَعُ المُهَنْدِسِينَ	كَتَبَ المُدِيرُ الرِّسَالَةَ إِلَى المُهَنْدِسِينَ
ذَهَبَ المُهَاجِرُونَ إِلَى المَدِينَةِ	نَصَرَ الأَنْصَارُ المُهَاجِرِينَ	كَانَ بِلَالٌ مِنَ المُهَاجِرِينَ

The sound feminine plural is a noun indicating three or more feminine persons or things. It is formed by adding the suffix ات to the singular the structure of which is maintained. The sound feminine plural will not have the vowel *fatha* in the accusative end-case, instead the accusative like the genitive is shown by the *kasrah* e.g.

المَرْفُوعُ	المَنْصُوبُ	المَجْرُورُ
جَاءَتْ المُسْلِمَاتُ	رَأَيْتُ المُسْلِمَاتِ	سَلَّمْتُ عَلَى المُسْلِمَاتِ
المُؤْمِنَاتُ صَائِمَاتٌ	خَاطَبَ اللهُ المُؤْمِنَاتِ	ذَهَبَ الرُّسُلُ إِلَى المُؤْمِنَاتِ
حَضَرَ المُعَلِّمَاتُ	سَأَلَ الطُّلَّابُ المُعَلِّمَاتِ	هَذِهِ كُتُبُ المُعَلِّمَاتِ
المُهَنْدِسَاتُ مُجْتَهِدَاتٌ	اسْتَأْجَرَ المَصْنَعُ	كَتَبَ المُدِيرُ الرِّسَالَةَ

	الْمُهَنْدِسَاتُ	إِلَى الْمُهَنْدِسَاتِ
ذَهَبَتِ الْمُهَاجِرَاتُ إِلَى الْمَدِينَةِ	نَصَرَ الْأَنْصَارُ الْمُهَاجِرَاتِ	هِيَ مِنَ الْمُهَاجِرَاتِ

The broken plural is the plural that does not retain the structure of its singular i.e. the singular is more or less altered by adding or decreasing its letters or changing its vowels. The broken plural has many patterns or scales on which it is formed. Since there is no specific rule as to which singular form is converted into which plural form, plurals of the *broken form* must be learnt and memorised by consulting a dictionary.

The following are some of the common patterns of the broken plural:

الوزن	الجمع	المفرد	الجمع	المفرد
أَفْعُلٌ	سَهْمٌ – أَسْهُمٌ		نَفْسٌ – أَنْفُسٌ	
أَفْعَالٌ	نَهْرٌ – أَنْهَارٌ		بَابٌ – أَبْوَابٌ	
أَفْعِلَةٌ	سُؤَالٌ – أَسْئِلَةٌ		جَوَابٌ – أَجْوِبَةٌ	
فُعُلٌ	سَفِينَةٌ – سُفُنٌ		كِتَابٌ – كُتُبٌ	
فُعُولٌ	شَهْرٌ – شُهُورٌ		قَلْبٌ – قُلُوبٌ	
فِعَالٌ	جَبَلٌ – جِبَالٌ		رَجُلٌ – رِجَالٌ	
أَفْعِلَاءُ	نَبِيٌّ – أَنْبِيَاءُ		صَدِيقٌ – أَصْدِقَاءُ	
فِعْلَانٌ	صَبِيٌّ – صِبْيَانٌ		غُلَامٌ – غِلْمَانٌ	
فُعَّالٌ	حَاكِمٌ – حُكَّامٌ		حَافِظٌ – حُفَّاظٌ	

شَرِيكٌ – شُرَكَاءُ	فَقِيرٌ – فُقَرَاءُ	فُعَلَاءُ
إصْبَعٌ – أَصَابِعُ	أَنْمِلَةٌ – أَنَامِلٌ	أَفَاعِلُ
إبْرِيقٌ – أَبَارِيقُ	إكْلِيلٌ – أَكَالِيلُ	أَفَاعِيلُ
مَسْجِدٌ – مَسَاجِدُ	مِنْبَرٌ – مَنَابِرُ	مَفَاعِلُ
مِصْبَاحٌ – مَصَابِيحُ	مِفْتَاحٌ – مَفَاتِيحُ	مَفَاعِيلُ

NOTE: Sometimes a noun will have more than one form of plural e.g.

شَهْرٌ – أَشْهُرُ / شُهُورُ

SUMMARY

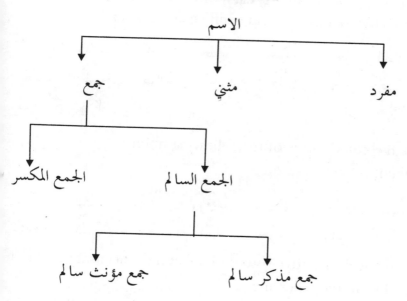

69

IMPORTANT TERMS

1) المفرد   The singular form.

2) المثنى   The dual form.

3) الجمع   The plural noun.

4) الجمع السالم   The sound plural.

5) الجمع المكسر   The broken plural.

6) جمع المذكر السالم   The sound masculine plural.

7) جمع المؤنث السالم   The sound feminine plural.

EXERCISE SIX

1) Give the dual form of each of the following nouns in the nominative, accusative and genitive end cases :

الخَادِمُ نَجَّارٌ الخَلِيفَةُ طَوِيْلٌ المَدِيْنَةُ مَدَرَسَةٌ مُدَرِّسٌ

عَيْنٌ جَزِيْرَةٌ دَارٌ حِمَارٌ صَالِحٌ صَاحِبٌ طَبِيْبٌ

إِمْرَأَةٌ نَهْرٌ

2) Give the plural forms of the following nouns:
(broken)

تِلْمِيْذٌ حَدِيْقَةٌ شَجَرَةٌ وَرَقٌ مَنْزِلٌ بِنْتٌ وَلَدٌ

قَمَرٌ رَأْسٌ بَحْرٌ مَدِيْنَةٌ أَسَدٌ كَلْبٌ نَافِذَةٌ

1) Form the nominative sound plural and the accusative sound plural from the following:

عَالِمٌ مُفْلِحٌ كَثِيْرٌ لاَعِبٌ مُجْتَهِدٌ حَاضِرٌ جَالِسٌ مُهَذَّبٌ

مُؤَدَّبٌ عَامِلٌ

70

2) Form the sound feminine plural from the following:

مُهَذَّبَةٌ   مُدَرِّسَةٌ   صَغِيرَةٌ   صَالِحَةٌ   ذَاكِرَةٌ ذَكِيَّةٌ   حَـــاضِرَةٌ

حَافِظَةٌ   كَلِمَةٌ   خَادِمٌ   عَابِدَةٌ   طَالِبَةٌ

3) Translate the following into English and underline all the singular, dual, and plural nouns:

{كَانَ النَّاسُ أُمَّةً وَاحِدَةً فَبَعَثَ اللَّهُ النَّبِيِّينَ مُبَشِّرِينَ وَمُنْذِرِينَ وَأَنْـــزَلَ مَعَـــهُمُ الْكِتَابَ بِالْحَقِّ لِيَحْكُمَ بَيْنَ النَّاسِ فِيمَا اخْتَلَفُوا فِيهِ وَمَا اخْتَلَفَ فِيهِ إِلاَّ الَّذِيـــنَ أُوتُوهُ مِنْ بَعْدِ مَا جَاءَتْهُمُ الْبَيِّنَاتُ بَغْياً بَيْنَهُمْ فَهَدَى اللَّهُ الَّذِينَ آمَنُوا لِمَا اخْتَلَفُوا فِيهِ مِنَ الْحَقِّ بِإِذْنِهِ وَاللَّهُ يَهْدِي مَنْ يَشَاءُ إِلَى صِرَاطٍ مُسْتَقِيمٍ} (البقرة:213)

Chapter Seven

المُركَّبُ : المُركَّبُ التَّوْصِيفِيُّ و المُركّبُ الإضَافِيُّ

The Composite: The Adjectival Composite And The Annexed Composite

In chapter one we said that two or more words make up a sentence. We went on to discuss in chapter two the meaningful composite e.g.

(الجُمْلَةُ الاسْميَّةُ) البنْتُ صَالِحَةٌ   ذَهَبَ زَيْدٌ (الجُمْلَةُ الفِعليةُ)

We also mentioned that some composites do not convey a complete meaning, and we called this category of composites المُركَّبُ غَيْر المُفِيْدِ. Here we will explore this concept in detail.

As discussed in chapter two, *the composite* or المركّب is a term used for a group of two or more words which may either convey a complete meaning, thereby forming a sentence, or convey an incomplete meaning, thereby forming a phrase (incomplete sentence). The complete sentence is called المُركَّبُ التَّامُ or what we termed (المُركَّبُ المُفِيْدُ). The incomplete sentence is called المُركَّبُ النَّاقِصُ , what we described as (المُركَّبُ غَيْر المُفِيْدِ). The incomplete sentence forms part of a sentence i.e. it may be the subject or the predicate or the doer or the direct object in the sentence.

The phrase - اَلْمَرَكَّبُ النَّاقِصُ – is further divided into two:

a) اَلْمُرَكَّبُ التَّوصِيفِيُّ   The adjectival composite

b) المَرَكَّبُ الإضَافِيُّ   The annexed composite

The adjectival composite or المركب التوصيفي is a construction of two words the second being an adjective, describing the first e.g.

A pious boy وَلَدٌ صَالِحٌ   The pious boy الولدُ الصَّالِحُ

A pious girl بِنْتٌ صَالِحَةٌ   The pious girl البِنْتُ الصَّالِحَةُ

The first noun is called مَوْصُوفٌ or the qualified noun (the noun being described). The second noun is called صِفَةٌ or the adjective (the describing word). The Arabic adjective follows the qualified noun, unlike in English where the adjective comes first e.g.

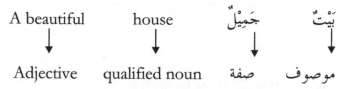

A beautiful	house	جَمِيلٌ	بَيْتٌ
↓	↓	↓	↓
Adjective	qualified noun	صفة	موصوف

The صفة must correspond with the موصوف in four aspects:

a) إعراب - end-case e.g.

جَاءَ الرَّجُلُ الطَّوِيلُ   The tall man came

رَأَيْتُ الرَّجُلَ الطَّوِيلَ   I saw the tall man

مَرَرْتُ بِالرَّجُلِ الطَّوِيلِ   I passed by the tall man

b) مذكر و مؤنث - gender e.g.

وَلَدٌ ذَكِيٌّ   A clever boy

بِنْتٌ ذَكِيَّةٌ   A clever girl

c) جمع , مثنّى , مفرد - number: singular, dual, plural e.g.

رَجُلٌ صَالِحٌ   A pious man (sing.)

رَجُلَانِ صَالِحَانِ   Two pious men (dual)

رِجَالٌ صَالِحُونَ   Pious men (plural)

d) معرفة , نكرة - definiteness and indefiniteness e.g.

بِنْتٌ مُجْتَهِدَةٌ   A hardworking girl

البِنْتُ المُجْتَهِدَةُ   The hardworking girl

The صفة for broken plurals of inanimate objects (غَيْرُ
ذَوِ العقول)   will be singular feminine e.g.

أَشْجَارٌ طَوِيلَةٌ   Tall trees

كُتُبٌ كَثِيرَةٌ   Many books

دُرُوسٌ سَهْلَةٌ   Easy lessons

بُيُوتٌ جَمِيلَةٌ   Beautiful houses

The basic differences between the موصوف and صفة and the
مبتدأ and خبر are as follows:

وَلَدٌ صَالِحٌ = المُرَكَّبُ التَّوْصِيفِيُّ A pious boy. (adjectival composite)

الوَلَدُ صَالِحٌ = الجُمْلَةُ الاسْمِيَّةُ The boy is pious. (nominal sentence)

The subject and predicate (the مبتدأ and خبر) form a complete
sentence while the موصوف and صفة are just part of a
sentence. Moreover, the مبتدأ and خبر conform in three
aspects only while the موصوف and صفة conform in four
aspects.

74

The المركّب الإضافي or annexed composite is a phrase consisting of two inter-related nouns connected together in such a way that the second noun possesses the first e.g.

كِتَابُ زَيْدٍ	Zaid's book
بَابُ البَيْتِ	The house's door
إِبْنُ المُعَلِّم	The teacher's son
ذَيْلُ الحِصَان	The horse's tail
مَدَرَسَةُ البَنَات	The Girls' school
رَسُولُ الله	The messenger of God
رَئِيسُ البَلَدِ	The president of the country
حَقِيبَةُ المُدَرِّس	The teacher's bag
جَامِعَةُ لَنْدَن	University of London

When translating the annexed composite into English the apostrophe ('s) as in "Zaid's book" or the preposition "of" as in " The book of Solomon " are generally used. The Arabic term for annexation is الإِضَافَة. The first part is called المُضَافُ and the second part is called المُضَافُ إليهِ e.g.

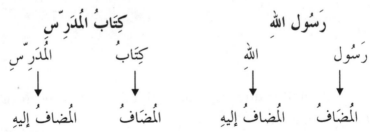

The مُضَافٌ can neither be prefixed by the definite article (ال) nor will it have the *tanwin* since the definite article is implied. It acquires definiteness by virtue of its annexation to the إليه

75

مُضَافٌ. The مُضَافٌ إليهِ on the other hand accepts both and it will always be in the genitive end-case (مَجْرُورٌ) e.g.

نُورُ الشَّمْسِ قَوِيٌّ   شَعَرُ البِنْتِ طَوِيلٌ   سَيَّارَةُ المُدِيرِ جَدِيْدَةٌ

It is a rule that the two annexed nouns should not be separated by any word. Consequently, if the مُضَافٌ is to be qualified with an adjective, the adjective must come after the مُضَافٌ إليهِ, and be prefixed with ال e.g.

The student's new book   كِتَابُ الطَّالِبِ الجَدِيْدُ

The king's beautiful daughter   بِنْتُ المَلِكِ الجَمِيْلَةُ

Some examples consist of more than one مُضَافٌ إليهِ i.e. the إليهِ مُضَافٌ plays a dual role, it will be a مضاف إليه for the word before it and a مضاف for the word after it e.g.

The colour of Muhammad's shirt.

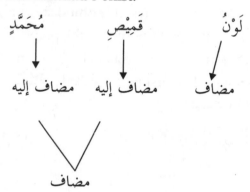

In the dual and sound masculine plurals the last *nun* is omitted if they appear as the مُضَافٌ e.g.

The man's two houses   بَيْتَا الرَّجلِ

The two daughters of the minister   إبْنَتَا الوَزِيرِ

The Secondary school's teachers   مُعَلِّمُو المَدْرَسَةِ الثَّانَوِيَّةِ

76

SUMMARY

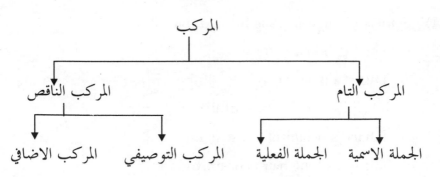

IMPORTANT TERMS

1) المركب — The Composite.

2) المركب التام — The complete composite.

3) المركب الناقص — The incomplete composite.

4) المركب التوصيفي — The adjectival composite.

5) المركب الاضافي — The annexed composite.

6) الموصوف — The qualified noun.

7) الصفة — The adjective.

8) غير عاقل — Inanimate object.

9) المضاف — The annexing noun.

10) المضاف إليه — The annexed noun.

EXERCISE SEVEN

1) Translate the following into Arabic:

   a) The big house is far

   b) This is a new car.

   c) Khalid's house is beautiful

   d) Khalid's beautiful house is far.

   e) The girl's long hair is beautiful

   f) The new books are in a small box.

   g) A good book and a short story

   h) The door of the man's house is open.

   i) The gardener is active

   j) The active gardener is in the market.

   k) In the wide river is cold water

   l) The tall trees are in a near garden.

   m) The new mosque of the city

   n) The windows of the mosque of the city are big

   o) The new mosque of the city

   p) The mosque of the new city.

   q) The door of Zaid's car is open

   r) The teachers of the school are present.

2. Translate into English:

   a) القَلَمُ الجَدِيدُ رَخِيصٌ

   b) قَلَمُ الوَلَدِ الجَدِيدِ رَخِيصٌ

c) قَلَمُ الوَلَدِ الجَدِيدُ رَخِيصٌ

d) هٰذَا مَيْدَانٌ فَسِيْحٌ

e) دَخَلْتُ المَدَرَسَةَ الجَدِيْدَةَ

f) قَرَأْتُ كِتَاباً مُفِيداً

g) مِفْتَاحُ بَابِ المَسْجِدِ فِي الحَقِيبَةِ

h) الطَّالِبَان الجَدِيْدَانِ مِنْ الكُوَيْتِ

i) مَرْيَمُ و سَلْمَى طَالِبَتَانِ مُجْتَهِدَتَان

j) أَقْرَأُ القُرْآنَ الكَرِيمَ كُلَّ صَبَّاحٌ

3) Correct the following:

i) بيتٌ محمدٌ صغيرةٌ

ii) بابُ البيتِ مغلقٍ

iii) ذَهَبْتُ إِلَى بيتٍ محمودٍ

iv) معلّمان المدرسةِ حاضِرَان

v) سَيارةُ الرجلِ الجديدةِ

vi) البَيْت الكبِيرُ الرجلِ

vii) الكتابُ الولدِ مفيدةٌ

viii) المِلِكُ عادلةٌ

ix) هذا بَيْتٌ قديمٌ

x) الطَّعامُ اللَّذِيْذَةَ

79

4)   Analyse the following sentences:

بابُ البيتِ مفتوحٌ

باب : مبتدأ , مرفوع , مضاف

البيت : مضاف إليه , مجرور

مفتوح : خبر , مرفوع . المبتدأ و الخبر= جملة اسمية

أَكَلَ زيدٌ تفاحةً لذيذةً

أكل : فعل ماض , مبني على الفتحة

زيد : فاعل , مرفوع

تفاحة : مفعول , منصوب و موصوف

لذِيذَةً : صفة , منصوب . الفعل و الفاعل = جملة اسمية

1) مُحَمَّدٌ رَسُوْلُ اللهِ   2) دَخَلْتُ المَدْرَسَةَ الجَدِيْدَةَ

3) قَرَأَ الطَّالَبُ كِتَاباً مُفِيداً   4) التِّلْمِيْذُ المُجْتَهِدُ نَاجِحٌ

5) جَاءَ الرّجُلُ الفَقِيْرُ   6) الكِتَابُ لِلطَّالِبِ الجَدِيْدِ

7) سَيّارَةُ ابْنِ المُدِيْرِ جَمِيْلَةٌ   8) بَابُ مَسْجِدِ المَدِيْنَةِ مَفْتُوْحٌ

9) شَعرُ البِنْتِ الجَمِيْلَةِ طَوِيْلٌ   10) يَلْعَبُ الأوْلَادُ فِي الحَدِيْقَةِ الجَمِيْلَةِ

Chapter Eight

الضَّمِيْرُ

The Personal Pronoun

The noun denoting the first, second, and the third persons is called ضَمِيْرٌ or the personal pronoun. They are fourteen in number:

	المؤنث	المذكر
غَائِب	هِيَ هُمَا هُنَّ	هُوَ هُمَا هُمْ
مُخَاطَب	أَنْتِ أَنْتُمَا أَنْتُنَّ	أَنْتَ أَنْتُمَا أَنْتُمْ
مُتَكَلِّم	أَنَا نَحْنُ	أنا نَحْنُ

The ضَمِيْرٌ is of two types:

a) الضَّمِيْرُ البَارِزُ - The prominent or visible pronoun: This pronoun is distinct and has its own visible form. It is pronounced either separately or attached to another word. e.g.

هو طالب	<u>He</u> is a student
هي طَالِبَةٌ	<u>She</u> is a student
أَنْتَ طَالِبٌ	<u>You</u> are a student (masc.)
أنتِ طالبة	<u>You</u> are a student (fem.)
نحن مُسْلِمُونَ	<u>We</u> are Muslims
إبْنُهُ مُجْتَهِدٌ	<u>His</u> son is hardworking
إبْنُهَا شُرْطِيٌّ	<u>Her</u> son is a policeman

هذا الِمفْتَاحُ لَك	The key is <u>for you</u>
نَصَرْتُهُ	<u>I</u> helped <u>him</u>
نَصَرْتُهَا	<u>I</u> helped <u>her</u>

b) الضّميرُ المُسْتَتِرُ - The hidden pronoun: This is not visible i.e. it is not written or pronounced and has no distinct form. It is *hidden* within the verb e.g.

الأمر	المضارع	الماضي
إذْهَبْ (أَنْتَ)	يَذْهَبُ (هو) تَذْهَبُ (هي) تَذْهَبُ (أنتِ) أَذْهَبُ (أنا) نَذْهَبُ (نحن)	ذَهَبَ (هو) ذَهَبَتْ (هي)

c) The الضمير البارز or prominent pronoun is further divided into two kinds:

الضمــير المُنْفَصِـلُ - The detached pronoun: This pronoun is written and pronounced separately from another word. i.e. it has its own exclusive form un-attached to another word e.g.

ضمائر النصب المنفصلة			ضمائر الرفع المنفصلة		
إيَّاهُ إيَّاهُمَا إيَّاهُمْ			هُوَ هُمَا هُمْ		
إيَّاهَا إيَّاهُمَا إيَّاهُنَّ			هِيَ هُمَا هُنَّ		
إيَّاكَ إيَّاكُمَا إيَّاكُمْ			أَنْتَ أَنْتُمَا انْتُمْ		
إيَّاكِ إيَّاكُمَا إيَّاكُنَّ			أَنْتِ أَنْتُمَا أَنْتُنَّ		
إيَّايَ إيَّانَا			أَنَا نَحْنُ		

d) الضَّمِيرُ المُتَّصِلُ - The attached pronoun: This pronoun is always attached or connected to another word i.e. it will be pronounced and written joined to either the verb as a direct object, to the noun to indicate possession, or to the preposition e.g.

ضمائر الجر المتصلة	ضمائر النصب المتصلة	ضمائر الرفع المتصلة
كِتَابُهُ – لَهُ	ضَرَبَهُ	-----
كِتَابُهُمَا – لَهُمَا	ضَرَبَهُمَا	كَتَبَا (ألف الاثنين)
كِتَابُهُمْ – لَهُمْ	ضَرَبَهُمْ	كَتَبُوا (واو الجمع)
كِتَابُهَا – لَهَا	ضَرَبَهَا	------
كِتَابُهُمَا – لَهُمَا	ضَرَبَهُمَا	كَتَبَتَا (ألف الاثنين)
كِتَابُهُنَّ – لَهُنَّ	ضَرَبَهُنَّ	كَتَبْنَ (نون النسوة)
كِتَابُكَ – لَكَ	ضَرَبَكَ	كَتَبْتَ (تاء الفاعل)
كِتَابُكُمَا – لَكُمَا	ضَرَبَكُمَا	كَتَبْتُمَا (تاء الفاعل)
كِتَابُكُمْ – لَكُمْ	ضَرَبَكُمْ	كَتَبْتُمْ (تاء الفاعل)
كِتَابُكِ – لَكِ	ضَرَبَكِ	كَتَبْتِ (تاء الفاعل)
كِتَابُكُمَا – لَكُمْ	ضَرَبَكُمَا	كَتَبْتُمَا (تاء الفاعل)
كِتَابُكُنَّ – لَكُنَّ	ضَرَبَكُنَّ	كَتَبْتُنَّ (تاء الفاعل)
كِتَابِي – لِي	ضَرَبَنِي	كَتَبْتُ (تاء الفاعل)
كِتَابُنَا – لَنَا	ضَرَبَنَا	كَتَبْنَا (نا الفاعلين)

As we mentioned in chapter three, all ضَمَائِر (pronouns) are indeclinable (مَبْنِي). The procedure when analysing sentences containing ضَمَائِر is as follows:

هُوَ طَالِبٌ:

هو : ضمير بارز منفصل مبني على الفتحة في محل الرفع = مبتدأ.

إِيَّاكَ نَعْبُدُ:

أياك : ضمير بارز منفصل مبني على الفتحة في محل النصب = مفعول
مقدم.

هَذَا كِتَابُهَا:

كتاب : خبر مرفوع و مضاف . ها : ضمير بارز متصل مبني على
الضمة في محل الجر , مضاف إليه

نَصَرْتُكَ:

نصرتك : ضمير بارز متصل مبني على الفتحة في محل النصب = مفعول به.

الكِتَابُ لَهَا:

لها : ضمير بارز متصل مبني على السكون في محل الجر.

The verb has its own pronoun and the pronoun will be بَارِزٌ or
نَائِبُ الْفَاعِلِ or فَاعِلٌ . The pronoun of a verb is either the مُسْتَتِرٌ
e.g.

ذَهَبَ : فعل ماض مبني على الفتحة , و الفاعل ضمير مستتر (هو)

ذَهَبَا : فعل ماض مبني على الفتحة و الفاعل ألف الاثنين.

أذْهَبُ : فعل مضارع مرفوع , و الفاعل ضمير مستتر (أنا)

نُصِرَتْ : فعل ماض مجهول , مبني على السكون و التاء تاء الفعل مبني على
الضمة في محل الرفع = نائب الفاعل

ضَرَبَتَنِي : فعل ماض مبني على السكون , و التاء تاء الفاعل مبني على الفتحة
في محل الرفع = فاعل , و النون نون الوقاية , و الياء ضمير بارز متصل مبني
على السكون في محل النصب = مفعول به

84

SUMMARY

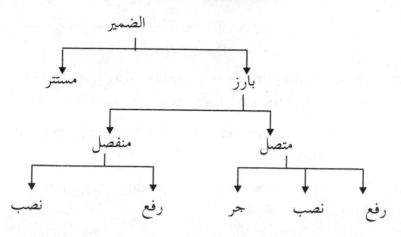

IMPORTANT TERMS

1)	الضمير	The Personal pronoun
2)	الضمير البارز	The Prominent pronoun
3)	الضمير المستتر	The Implied pronoun
4)	الضمير المنفصل	The detached pronoun
5)	الضمير المتصل	The Attached pronoun

EXERCISE EIGHT

1. Define each of the following terms and provide examples in form of complete sentences:

الضمير المستتر   الضمير البارز   الضمير

الضمير المنفصل   الضمير المتصل

85

2. Translate the following into Arabic:

    i) The two boys' names are Hamid and Mahmud , and the two girls' names are Zainab and Aishah.

    ii) This is Sumayyah, she is a hardworking student , and these are her friends , they are students in her school.

    iii) This is my friend Zaid, and this is his house, its garden is beautiful.

    iv) These two students are hard working, they are from Africa.

    v) The teacher wrote the lesson on the board and explained it.

    vi) We helped them (plural. masc.) and you (plural.masc.) helped us.

    vii) My mother hit me so I cried.

    viii) For you (plural. masc.) is your religion and for me is my religion.

    ix) The principal is in his office , you (sing.masc.) must go to him.

    x) The boys and their friends went to the mosque.

3. Translate the following into English:

عَنْ ابْنِ عُمَرَ رضي الله عَنْهُمَا قَالَ: قَالَ رَسُولُ اللّهِ صَلَّى اللهُ عليهِ وآلِهِ
وسَلَّم : بُنِيَ الإِسْلَامُ عَلَى خَمْس: شَهَادَة أَنْ لا إِلهَ إلاَّ اللّهُ وأَنَّ مُحَمَّداً
رَسُولُ اللّهِ، و إقَامِ الصَّلاةِ، وإيتَاءِ الزَّكَاةِ، والْحَجِّ، وصَوْمِ رَمَضَـــانَ.
رواه البخاري

Chapter Nine

إِسْمُ الإِشَارَةِ

The Demonstrative Pronoun

The term الإِشَارَة literally means "signal", "gesture", "indication" and it is derived from the radicals شور and the verb أَشَارَ which means "to point out", "to signal" etc. The demonstrative pronoun (إِسْمُ الإِشَارَةِ) is a word used to demonstrate or point out an object or person e.g.

هَذَا بَيْتٌ	This is a house
هَذِه مَدْرَسَةٌ ابْتِدَائِيَّةٌ	This is a primary school
ذَلِكَ طَبِيبٌ	That is a doctor
تِلْكَ امْرَأَةٌ	That is a woman

There are two kinds of demonstrative pronouns:

a) إِسْمُ الإِشَارَةِ لِلْقَرِيْبِ   The *demonstrative noun* for near objects

b) إِسْمُ الإِشَارَةِ لِلْبَعِيْدِ   The *demonstrative noun* for distant objects

بَعِيْدٌ - Distant	قَرِيبٌ - Near
ذلك تلك	هذا هذه
ذانك / ذينك تانك / تينك	هذان / هذين هاتان / هاتين
أولائك	هؤلاء

The noun to which the demonstration is made is called the مُشَارٌ إِليه. The إِسْمُ الإِشَارَةِ and the مُشَارُ إِليه together make up a complete sentence الْمُرَكَّبُ التَّامُّ when the مُشَارٌ إِليه is نَكِرَةٌ e.g.

هَذَا كِتَابٌ

هذا : اسم الإشارة , مبني على السكون في محل الرفع = مبتدأ.

كتاب : المُشَارُ إليهِ ، خبر مرفوع.

المُبتدأ و الخبر= الجملة الاسمية.

When the إليـــهِ مُشَارٌ is مَعْرِفَةٌ , the إسْمُ الإشَارَةِ and مُشَارٌ إليهِ will make up a phrase or incomplete sentence (المُرَكَّبُ النَّاقِصُ). In such a case they form part of a complete sentence. The مُشَارٌ إليـــهِ in this instance is termed البَدَلُ (appositional substantive standing for another substantive) and will have the same end case as the إسْمُ الإشَارَةِ e.g.

هَذَا الكِتَابُ جَدِيدٌ

هذا : إسم الإشارة مبني على السكون في محل الرفع= مبتدأ الكتاب :
بدَل مرفوع.

جديد : خبر مرفوع.

المبتدأ و الخبر= جملة اسمية.

قَرَأتُ هَذَا الكِتَابَ.

قرأت : فعل ماض مبني على السكون , و التاء تاء الفاعل، ضمير بارز
متصل مبني على الضمة في محل الرفع= فاعل.

الفعل و الفاعل= جملة فعلية.

هذا : اسم الإشارة مبني على السكون في محل النصب، مفعول به.

الكتاب : بدل منصوب.

قَرَأتُ فِي هَذَا الكِتَاب.

قرأت : فعل ماض مبني على السكون , و التاء تاء الفاعل , ضمير بارز
متصل مبني على الضمة في محل الرفع =فاعل.

الفعل و الفاعل= الجملة الفعلية.

في : حرف الجر مبني على السكون.

هذا : اسم الإشارة مبني على السكون في محل الجر

الكتاب : بدل مجرور.

ذَهَبَ هَذَا الطَّالِبُ إِلَى المَدْرَسَةِ.

ذهب : فعل ماض مبني على الفتحة

هذا : اسم الإشارة مبني على السكون في محل الرفع= فاعل.

الفعل و الفاعل= جملة فعلية.

الطالب : بدل مرفوع

إلى: حرف الجر مبني على السكون

المدرسة : اسم مجرور.

ابْنُ هَذَا الرَّجُلِ مُطِيعٌ.

ابن : مبتدأ مرفوع و مضاف

هذا : اسم الإشارة مبني على السكون في محل الجر= مضاف إليه

الرجل : بدل مجرور

مطيع : خبر مرفوع . المبتدأ و الخبر= جملة اسمية.

The إِسْمُ الإِشَارَةِ and مُشَارٌ إِلَيهِ must conform in gender and number, and the singular feminine (هَـذِهِ) is used for demonstrating the plural of inanimate objects (غير ذَوِ العُقُول) e.g.

هَذَا وَلَدٌ – هَذَانِ وَلَدَانِ – هَؤُلَاءِ أَوْلَادٌ

هَذَا كِتَابٌ – هَذَانِ كِتَابَانِ – هَذِهِ كُتُبٌ

هَذِهِ بِنْتٌ – هَاتَانِ بِنْتَانِ – هَؤُلَاءِ بَنَاتٌ

هَذِهِ شَجَرَةٌ – هَاتَانِ شَجَرَتَانِ – هَذِهِ أَشْجَارٌ

ذَلِكَ رَجُلٌ   -   ذَانِكَ رَجُلَانِ   -   أُولَئِكَ رِجَالٌ

تِلْكَ امْرَأَةٌ   -   تَانِكَ امْرَأَتَانِ   -   أُولَئِكَ نِسَاءٌ

ذَلِكَ بَيْتٌ   -   ذَانِكَ بَيْتَانِ   -   تِلْكَ بُيُوتٌ

تِلْكَ مَدَرَسَةٌ - تَانِكَ مَدَرَسَتَانِ - تِلْكَ مَدَارِسٌ

When a مُضَافٌ is the object of demonstration the إِسْمُ
الإِشَارَةِ must be mentioned after the مُضَافٌ إِلَيهِ e.g.

This son of the principal is obedient.   إِبنُ المُدِيرِ هَذَا مُطِيعٌ

This book of yours is beneficial   كِتَابُكَ هَذَا مُفِيْدٌ

These windows of the Mosque are   نَوَافِـذُ المسْـجِدِ هَـذِهِ
opened.   مَفْتُوحَةٌ

This religion of ours is beautiful.   دِينُنَا هَذَا جَمِيْلٌ

The أَسْمَاءُ الاشَارَة (demonstrative pronouns) are indeclinable, with
the exception of the dual forms which are declinable e.g.

هذان كتابَانِ (مرفوع)   These are two books

قرأتُ هذَيْنِ الكِتَابَيْنِ (منصوب)   I read these two books

كَتَبْتُ في هَذَيْنِ الكِتَابَيْنِ (مجرور)   I wrote in these two books

The nouns هُنَـا (here)   and هُنَاكَ (there)   are also from the
category of أسماء الإشارة. They denote place, near and distant
e.g.

هُنَا بَيْتُ مُحَمَّدٍ   Here is Muhammad's house

هُنَاكَ مَدَرَسَةُ مُحَمَّدٍ   There is Muhammad's school

IMPORTANT TERMS

1) اسم الإشارة   The demonstrative pronoun

2) اسم الإشارة للقريب   The demonstrative pronoun for near objects

3) اسم الإشارة للبعيد   The demonstrative pronoun for distant objects

4) المشار إليه   The object of the demonstration

5) البدل   The substitute

EXERCISE NINE

1) Give examples of the following in complete sentences:

البدل   اسم الإشارة للبعيد   المشار إليه   اسم الإشارة للقريب   اسم الإشارة

2) Translate the following into Arabic:

    i)   These flowers are beautiful and those trees are tall.

    ii)   What is the colour of this house? Its colour is white.

    iii)   This daughter of yours (sing. fem) is intelligent.

    iv)   I took the two books and two pens from this bag.

    v)   That man is the Imam of this mosque.

    vi)   This brother of yours (sing. masc.) is the principal of that secondary school.

    vii)   These men are Muslims, they are doctors and those women are Muslims, they are Professors at the Islamic University.

viii)   These two girls are sisters. They are students in the primary school.

ix)   These are two pens; they are for those two students. (masc.)

x)   Here is my school and there is my house.

3) Translate the following to English:

2) هذا الولدُ صالحٌ   1) هذا ولدٌ صالحٌ

4) هذا ابنُ المديرِ   3) ولَدُكَ صالحٌ

6) ابنُ المديرِ هذا ذكيٌّ   5) ابنُ هذا المديرِ ذكيٌّ

4) Analyse the following sentences:

1) خَرَجَ هذا الطالبُ من الفصلِ   2) اسم هذه البنتِ سَلْمَى

5) Translate the following into English:

عن علي بن أبي طالب رضي الله عنه قال: إنَّ رَسُولَ اللّه صَلَّى اللّه عليهِ وآلِهِ وسَلَّم أَخَذَ حَرِيراً، فَجَعَلَهُ في يَمِينِهِ، وأَخَذَ ذَهَباً فَجَعَلَهُ في شِمَالِهِ، ثُمَّ قَالَ: إنَّ هَذَيْنِ حَرَامٌ عَلَى ذُكُورِ أُمَّتِي. رَوَاهُ أحمدٌ وأبُو دَاوُد والنَّسَائِي

Chapter Ten

إِسْمُ المَوصُولِ

The Relative Pronoun

The relative pronoun or إِسْمُ المَوصُولِ is a word which has a relation or connection to the sentence following it. The sentence following such a noun may be nominal or verbal and is called صِلَةُ المَوصُولِ. The relative pronouns (الأَسْمَاءُ المَوصُولَةُ) are:

جمع - Plural	مثنَّى - Dual	مفرد -Singular
الَّذِينَ (مُذَكَّرٌ)	الَّذان / اللَّذَيْنِ (مُذَكَّرٌ)	الَّذِي (مُذَكَّرٌ)
اللاَّتِي / اللاَّئِي (مُؤَنَّثٌ)	اللَّتَانِ / اللَّتَيْنِ (مُؤَنَّثٌ)	الَّتِي (مُؤَنَّثٌ)

The relative pronoun مَــا is used for objects and non-humans while the relative pronoun مَنْ is exclusively for humans.

الَّذِي كَتَبَ الدَّرسَ عَلَى السَّبُّورة محمدٌ

الَّتِي كَتَبَتْ الدَّرسَ عَلَى السَّبُّورة خَدِيْجَةٌ

اللَّذان كَتَبَا الدَّرسَ عَلَى السبورة محمدٌ و خديجةٌ

اللَّتان كَتَبَتَا الدَّرسَ عَلَى السَّبُّورة فاطِمَةُ و مريمُ

الَّذين كَتَبُوا الدَّرسَ عَلَى السَّبُّورة محمدٌ و زيدٌ و يُوسُفُ

اللاَّتِي كَتَبْنَ الدَّرسَ عَلَى السَّبُّورة عائشة و مريمُ و خديجةٌ

اللهُ يَعْلَمُ مَا تَفْعَلُونَ

اللهُ يَعْلَمُ مَنْ يَعْبُدُهُ

The إسْمُ المَوْصُول صِلَةُ should have a ضَمِيرٌ which refers to the إسْمُ المَوْصُول. This ضَمِيرٌ is called عَائِدٌ ضَمِيرٌ and conforms with the إسْمُ المَوْصُولَ in number and gender e.g.

الكِتَابُ الّذي قَرَأتُهُ مُفِيدٌ

الكِتَابَان اللّذَان قَرَأتُهُمَا مُفِيدَان

الكُتُبُ الّتِي قَرَأتَهَا مُفِيدَةٌ

الطّالِبَةُ الّتِي خَرَجَتْ مِنَ الفَصْلِ مِن الكُوَيْت

الطّالِبَتَان اللّتَان خَرَجَتَا مِنَ الفَصْلِ مِنَ الكُوَيت

الطّالِبَاتْ الّلاتِي خَرَجْنَ مِنَ الفَصْلِ مِنَ الكُوَيْت

The صِلَةِ المَوْصُول may be nominal or verbal sentence e.g.

حَضَرَ اللّذِينَ هُمْ أصْدِقَائِي (الجملة الاسمية)

الرّجالُ اللّذِينَ يَجلِسُونَ فِي الفَنَاء عُلَمَاءُ. (الجملة الفعلية)

The صِلَةِ المَوْصُولِ may also be شِبْهُ الجُمْلَةِ or a *quasi* sentence e.g.

قَطَفْتُ الأزْهَارَ الّتِي فِي الحَدِيقَةِ. (جار و بجرور = شِبْهُ الجُمْلَةِ)

أُنْظُرْ إلَى السّيَّارَةِ الّتِي أَمَامَ المَسْجِدِ. (ظرف ومضاف إليه = شِبْهُ الجُمْلَةِ)

The أسْمَاءُ المَوْصُولَةِ are indeclinable with the exception of the dual form e.g.

قَرَأتُ المَجَلّتَيْنِ اللّتَيْنِ هُمَا فِي المَكْتَبَةِ (منصوب)

جَلَسَ الطّالِبَان عَلَى المَقْعَدَيْنِ اللّذَيْنِ أمَامَ المُدَرّسِ (بجرور)

سَافَرَ الطّبِيبَان اللّذَان مِنْ أفريقيا (مرفوع)

IMPORTANT TERMS

1) إسم الموصول   The Relative pronoun

2) صلة الموصول   The sentence following the relative pronoun

3) ضمير عائد   Returning personal pronoun

4) شبه الجملة   Quasi sentence.

EXERCISE TEN

1) Define the following with examples:

شبه الجملة   ضمير عائد   صلة الموصول   إسم الموصول

2) Translate the following into Arabic:

i)   The car which you bought is beautiful.

i)   Those (plural.masc.) who went to India are scholars from the university.

iii)   I know what you wrote and I understood it.

iv)   Eat from that which is in front of you.

v)   I took the two apples which you bought

vi)   The women who wrote this book are teachers in our school

vii) The tree which is behind my house is big.

viii) Those who are going to the market are traders from Africa.

ix) I wrote the two lessons which the teacher explained yesterday.

x) The students (plural. fem) from this university are hardworking.

3) Analyse the following:

1- الذي دخل المصنع مهندس

2- رأيت الطالبين اللذين خرجا من الفصل

3- الكتاب الذي قرأته قيم

4- أنظر إلى السيارة التي أمامك

1) Translate the following into English:

عن عائشة قالت: تلا رسول الله صلى الله عليه وآله وسلم {هو الذي أنـــزل عليك الكتاب منه آيات محكمات هن أم الكتاب وأخر متشاهـــات فأمـــا الذين في قلوبهم زيغ فيتبعون ما تشابه منه ابتغاء الفتنة وابتغاء تأويله وما يعلم تأويله إلا الله والراسخون في العلم يقولون آمنا به كل من عند ربنا وما يذكر إلا أولو الألباب}. قالت: قال رسول الله صلى الله عليه وآله وسلم: إذا رأيتم الذين يتبعون ما تشابه منه فأولئك الذين سمي الله فاحذروهم.   رَواه مسلم

Chapter Eleven

الصَّحِيْحُ و غَيْرُ الصَّحِيْحِ الاسمُ

The Regular And Irregular Noun

The Arabic noun is subdivided into two categories with respect to its root letters. The noun having no defective letters (حُرُوفُ العِلَّةِ) nor *hamzah* as its final radical, is called *the regular noun* or الاسْمُ الصَّحِيْحُ e.g.

رَجُلٌ   بَيْتٌ   كِتَابٌ

The noun having a defective letter as its final radial or *hamzah* is called إِسْمُ غَيْرِ صَحِيْحٍ or *the irregular noun*. The defective letters are ى – ا – و e.g.

(ي)   الرَّاعِي   القَاضِي   الوَادِي

بُشْرَى   حُبْلَى   مُسْتَشْفَى (اِلِفٌ مَقْصُورَةٌ)

سَمَاء   صَحْرَاء   كَهْرَبَاء (اِلِفٌ مَمْدُودَةٌ)

The irregular noun is further divided into three categories:

    i) الاسْمُ المَنْقُوصُ   The defective noun

   ii) الاسْمُ المَقْصُورُ   The abbreviated noun

  iii) الاسْمُ المَمْدُودُ   The extended noun

The defective noun or الاسْمُ المَنْقُوصُ is the noun having the letter ي (*yaa*) as its final radial when the letter preceding the *yaa* has a *kasrah* .e.g.

الرَّامِيْ   الهَادِيْ   المُحَامِيْ

The vowels of the *yaa* of the defective noun are not visible when it is prefixed by the definite article, only the *fatha* will be visible, and a *sukun* takes the place of the *dammah* and *kasrah* e.g.

حَضَرَ القَاضِيْ (فاعل , مرفوع)

نَظَرْتُ إلى القَاضِيْ (مجرور بإلى)

رَأَيْتُ القَاضِيَ (مفعول به , منصوب)

The ي (*yaa*) will be deleted from the defective noun when it has the nunation (تنويــــن) (تنويــن) in the case when it is مرفوع and مجـــرور. However, in cases when it is in the accusative form (منصوب) it will retain the ي e.g.

حَضَرَ قَاضٍ   نَظَرْتُ إلَى قَاضٍ   رَأَيْتُ قَاضِياً

The dual and the plural of the defective noun is as follows:

قَاضٍ – قَاضِيَان – قُضَاةٌ   رَاعٍ – رَاعِيَان – رُعَاةٌ

دَاعٍ – دَاعِيَان – دُعَاةٌ   مُحَامٍ – مُحَامِيَان – مُحَامُونَ

مُنَادٍ – مُنَادِيَان – مُنَادُونَ   بَاغٍ – بَاغِيَان – بَاغُونَ

The abbreviated noun or الاسم المقصور is the noun having the shortened *alif* or ألف مقصورة as its final radical when the letter preceding the *alif* has a *fatha*. e.g.

العَصَا   الدُّنْيَا   الهُدَى   الفَتَى

None of the three vowels of the *alif* of the abbreviated noun are visible e.g.

جَاءَ الفَتَى (فاعل مرفوع)

نَظَرْتُ إلى الفَتَى (مجرور)

رَأَيْتُ الفَتَى (مفعول به منصوب)

The dual and plural forms of the abbreviated noun are as follows:

أُخْرَيَاتٌ	أُخْرَيَانِ	أُخْرَى
أَعْلُونَ	أَعلِيانِ	أَعْلَى
حُسْنَيَاتٌ	حُسْنَيَانِ	حُسْنَى
فَتَاوَى	فَتْوَيَانِ	فَتْوَى
فِتْيَةٌ	فَتَيَانِ	فَتَى
مُسْتَشْفَيَاتٌ	مُسْتَشْفَيَانِ	مُسْتَشْفَى

The extended noun or الاســـم الممــــدود is the noun having the extended *alif* or ألف ممدودة as its final radical . e.g.

بِنَاءٌ	خَضْرَاءُ	إِنْشَاءٌ	كِسَاءٌ
مَسَاءٌ	أَقْرِبَاءُ	عُلَمَاءُ	دُعَاءٌ

IMPORTANT TERMS

1. الاسم الصحيح	The regular noun
2. الاسم غير الصحيح	The irregular noun
3. الاسم المنقوص	The defective noun
4. الاسم المقصور	The abbreviated noun
5. الاسم الممدود	The extended noun
6. حروف العلة	The defective letters

EXERCISE ELEVEN

1) State what is meant by the following terms. Provide examples.

1) الاسم الصحيح   2) الاسم غير الصحيح   3) الاسم المنقوص

4) الاسم المقصور   5) الاسم الممدود

2)   Translate the following passage and rewrite it with the correct diacritical points:

عن أبي سعيد الخدري أن نبي الله صلى الله عليه وآله وسلم قال: كان فيمن كان قبلكم رجل قتل تسعه وتسعين نفسا فسأل عن أعلم أهل الأرض فدل على راهب فأتاه فقال إنه قتل تسعة وتسعين نفسا فهل له من توبة فقال لا فقتله فكمل به مائة ثم سأل عن أعلم أهل الأرض فدل على رجل عالم فقال إنه قتل مائة نفس فهل له من توبة فقال نعم ومن يحول بينه وبين التوبة انطلق إلى أرض كذا وكذا فإن بهـــا أناسا يعبدون الله فاعبد الله معهم ولا ترجع إلى أرضك فإنها أرض سوء فـــأنطلق حتى إذا نصف الطريق أتاه الموت فاختصمت فيه ملائكة الرحمة وملائكة العـــذاب فقالت ملائكة الرحمة جاء تائبا مقبلا بقلبه إلى الله وقالت ملائكة العذاب إنـــه لم يعمل خيرا قط فأتاهم ملك في صورة آدمي فجعلوه بينهم فقال قيسوا مـــا بـــين الأرضين فإلى أيتهما كان أدنى فهو له فقاسوه فوجدوه أدنى إلى الأرض الـــتي أراد فقبضته ملائكة الرحمة قال قتادة فقال الحسن ذكر لنا أنه لما أتاه الموت نأى بصدره. رواه مسلم

Chapter Twelve

المَمْنُوعُ مِنَ الصَّرْفِ

The Un-Nunated Noun

In chapter three we discussed the declinable and indeclinable nouns. We said that the declinable nouns are those nouns whose last radicals change according to their grammatical position in a sentence. We then defined the indeclinable nouns as those whose last radicals refuse to change in spite of of their grammatical position. In this chapter we will discuss in detail another category of declinable nouns.

The declinable noun is subdivided into two categories:

a) الاسمُ المُنْصَرِفُ   The Nunated noun

b) المَمْنُوعُ مِنَ الصَّرْفِ   The un – Nunated noun

The nunated noun or الاسم المنصرف is the noun that accepts *tanwin* or nunation and all the vowels showing the end-case are visible .e.g.

كِتَاباً   كِتَابٍ   كِتَابٌ

The un-nunated noun or الاسْمُ المَمْنُوعُ مِنَ الصَّرْفِ is the noun that does not accept the *tanwin* or *kasrah* , instead a *fatha* will be the sign of جَرٌّ (genitive) e.g.

رَأَيْتُ يُوسُفَ (نصب)   هَذَا يُوسُفُ (رفع)

الغِلَافُ أَحْمَرُ (رفع)   هذا الكِتَابُ لِيُوسُفَ (جرّ)

الكِتَابُ في غِلَافٍ أَحْمَرَ (جرّ)   إِشْتَرَيْتُ ثَوباً أَحْمَرَ (نصب)

The un-nunated noun will only accept a *kasrah* in the following two instances:

i) When prefixed with the definite article. e.g.

الكتاب في الغلافِ الأحمر   يَعِيشُ الأعْرابُ في الصَّحْراء

b) When it is مضاف e.g.

ذَهَبْتُ إلى أفْضَلِ العُلَماء   الجَائِزَةُ لأكْبَرِ التَّلامِيذِ

The un-nunated nouns are confined to the following categories of nouns:

1. The simple proper noun (العَلَمُ المُفْرَدُ) . These are:

a) Proper nouns ending with *alif* and *nun*(ان) e.g

مَرْوَانُ – عَدْنَانُ – سُلَيْمَانُ – عُثْمَانُ

لُقْمَانُ – نُعْمَانُ – شَعْبَانُ – رَمَضَانُ

b) Proper nouns of females, or the names of males that end with تاء المربوطة e.g.

عائشةُ – فاطمةُ – مَكةُ – مريمُ – زينبُ

حذيفةُ – عبيدةُ – طلحةُ – معاويةُ – حمزةُ

c) Foreign Arabicised names e.g.

إسْحَاقُ جِبْرِيلُ إدْرِيسُ يَعْقُوبُ إبْرَاهِيْمُ إسْمَاعِيلُ مِيكائيلُ

d) Proper nouns on the scales أفْعَل and يَفْعَل and يَفْعِلُ e.g.

أكْرُمُ – أسْلَمُ – أنْوَرُ – أحْمَدُ

مُضَرُ – قُزَحُ – زُفَرُ – عُمَرُ

يَعْرُبُ – يَنْبَعُ – يَثْرِبُ – يَزِيدُ

2. The un-nunated adjective (الصِّفَةُ المَمْنُوعَةُ مِنَ الصَّرْفِ). These are:

a) Adjectives on the scale فَعْلَانُ with the feminine on the scale فُعْلَى e.g.

عَطْشَانُ - عَطْشَى   سَكْرَانُ   سَكْرَى   جَوعَانُ -
جَوعَى   شَبْعَانُ   -   شَبْعَى

b) The adjective on the scale أَفْعَلُ with the feminine on the scale فُعلى or فَعْلَاءُ e.g.

أحْمَرُ - حُمَراءُ   أَزْرَقُ - زَرْقَاءُ   أخضرُ - خَضْرَاءُ
أكْبَرُ - كُبْرَى   أحْسَنُ - حُسْنَى   أصْغَرُ - صُغْرَى

c) Some abbreviated and extended nouns (مَقْصُورٌ / مَمْدُودٌ) e.g.

حُبْلَى   بُشْرَى   ذِكْرَى   سَلْوَى
صَحْرَاءُ   سَوْدَاءُ   كَهْرَبَاءُ   أصْدِقَاءُ

d) The ultimate plural or مُنْتَهَى الجُمُوع : The two scales of the broken plural. These plurals appear on the scales of مَفَاعِلُ مَفَاعِيْلُ e.g.

مَفَاعِلُ : مَسَاجِدُ ، مَدَارِسُ ، أكَارِمُ ، شَوَارِعُ ، رَسَائِلُ
مَفَاعِيْلُ : مَصَابِيْحُ ، مَفَاتِيْحُ ، أناشِيْدُ ، قَنَابِيْلُ ، أبَارِيقُ

IMPORTANT TERMS

1) الاسم المنصرف	The Nunated noun	
2) الاسم الممنوع من الصرف	The Un-nunated noun	
3) منتهى الجموع	The Ultimate plural	

EXERCISE TWELVE

1) State what is meant by each of the following:

a) الاسم المنصرف

b) الممنوع من الصرف

2) Translate the following passage and rewrite it in its correct diacritical points:

عن البراء قال: ما رأيت من ذي لمة في حلة حمراء أحسن من رسول الله صلى الله عليه وآله وسلم له شعر يضرب منكبيه بعيد ما بــــين المنكبــــين لم يكـــن بالقصير ولا بالطويل. رَواه الترمذي

Chapter Thirteen

الحُرُوف

The Particles

In chapter one, we defined particles as those words that are dependent on the noun or verb in order to convey a complete and useful meaning. We went on to give a few examples of particles and since they are many types of particles in Arabic used for different purposes, explaining all of them in chapter one would have been pre-mature considering the fact that one needs to learn certain basic grammar laws that are a pre-requisite for comprehending all the categories of particles. Since we are confident that you have leant in the previous chapters most of such basic grammar laws, we see it fit to discuss in the next chapters all the other categories we could not explain in chapter one.

The particles are divided into two categories:

a) حُرُوفُ المَبَاني   or the letters of construction

b) حُرُوفُ المَعَاني   or the letters of significance (the particles)

The letters of construction are the letters of the Arabic alphabet also termed الحُـــرُوفُ الهِجَائِيَـــة. They are twenty-nine in number commencing from the *hamzah* and ending at the ي (*yaa*). These letters are used in the construction of words e.g.

ق - ل - م (قَلَمٌ)   ج - ل - س (جَلَسَ)

م - ن (مِنْ)

The letters of construction falls under two categories; *sun letters* and *moon letters* which we have discussed in detail in chapter chapter four.

The term حُرُوفُ المَعَاني is used to refer to the particles which we use in sentences. Their meaning becomes clear when they are used along with nouns or verbs in a sentence e.g.

لَمْ تَحْضُرْ زينبُ في الفصل   Zainab was not present in the class.

Some particles effect the end-cases of the noun or the verb they appear before and such particles are called الحروفُ العَامِلَةُ or *causative particles*. Others do not have the same effect on the end-case of the word they appear before and we call such particles حروف غَيرعَامِلةٍ or *non-causative particles* e.g.

إنَّ الكِتَابَ مُفِيْدٌ (عَامِلَةٌ) Indeed the book is beneficial

هَلْ الكتَابُ مُفِيْدٌ؟ (غَيرعَامِلةٍ) Is the books beneficial?

When you look at the first example above, you will see that the word الكِتَــاب appearing after the underlined particle إنَّ has a *fatha* to indicate that it is *accusative*. The presence of this particle has affected the end-case of the word الكِتَاب . The particle إنَّ therefore is a *causative particle*. In the second example you will see that the presence of the particle هَل before the word الكِتَاب has not affected the word in any way. This shows that the particle هَل belongs to the category of the *non-causative particles*.

The causative particles or حُرُوفُ عَامِلَةٍ are of three types :

a) حُرُوفُ الجَرِّ - The prepositions: These particles, seventeen in number, only appear before nouns. The noun following any of these particles will be مَجْرُورٌ (genitive) i.e it will have a *kasrah* as the end-case. This noun is thereafter called الاسمُ المَجْرُورُ or the *genitive noun*.

The prepositions are:

ب ، تَ ، كَ ، لِ ، وَ ، مُنْذُ ، مُذ ، خَلاَ ، رُبَّ

حَاشَا ، مِنْ ، عَدَا ، فِي ، عَنْ ، عَلَى ، حَتَّى ، إلَى

b) حُرُوفُ النَّصْبِ - The subjunctive particles: These particles are ten in number, six of these appear before nouns and four before the present tense verb. The noun or verb following any of these particles will be مَنْصُوبٌ i.e. it will have a *fatha* as the end-case.

The Subjunctive Particles are:

إنَّ ، أنَّ ، لَكِنَّ ، لَعَلَّ ، لَيْتَ ، كَأَنَّ ، - (اسم)

أنْ ، لَنْ ، كَيْ ، إذَنْ - (فعل مضارع)

c) حُرُوفُ الجَزْمِ - The jussive particles: These particles are five in number. They only appear before the present tense verb. The verb following any of these particles will be مَجْزُومٌ i.e. it will have a *sukun* (anti-vowel) as the end-case .The jussive particles are:

إنْ ، لَمْ ، لَمَّا ، لِ ، لا

SUMMARY

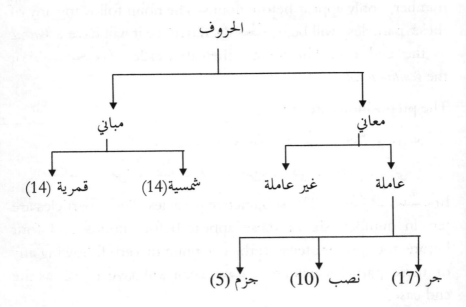

IMPORTANT TERMS

1- حروف المباني   The letters of construction

2- حروف المعاني   The letters of significance (The Particles)

3- الحروف الهجائية   The letters of the alphabet

4- حروف عاملة   Causative Particles

5- حروف عاطلة   Non-Causative particles

6- حروف الجر   The Prepositions

7- حروف النصب   The Subjunctive particles

8- حروف الجزم   The Jussive particles

EXERCISE THIRTEEN

1. Translate the following passage and underline all the particles:

كانت عند العرب بقايا من الحنيفية التي ورثوها من دين إبراهيم عليــه الســلام، فكانوا مع –ما هم عليه من الشرك– يتمسكون بأمور صحيحة توارثها الأبناء عن الآباء كابراً عن كابر، وكان بعضهم أكثر تمسكاً بها من بعض، بل كانت طائفة منهم –وهم قلة– تعاف وترفض ما كان عليه قومها من الشرك وعبادة الأوثان، وأكل الميتة، ووأد البنات، ونحو ذلك من العادات التي لم يأذن بها الله، ولم يأت بها شرع حنيف، وكان من تلك الطائفة ورقة بن نوفل و زيد بن نفيل ورسولنا صلى الله عليه وآله وسلم ، والذي امتاز عن غيره صلى الله عليه وآله وسلم باعتزالــه الناس للتعبد والتفكُّر في غار حراء. كان النبي صلى الله عليه وسلم يتأمل منـــذ صغره ما كان عليه قومه من العبادات الباطلة والأوهام الزائفة، التي لم تجد سـبيلاً إلى نفسه، ولم تلق قبولاً في عقله، بسبب ما أحاطه الله من رعاية وعناية لم تكــن لغيره من البشر، فبقيت فطرته على صفائها، تنفر من كل شيء غير ما فطــرت عليه.

هذا الحال الذي كان عليه صلى الله عليه وآله وسلم دفع به إلى اعتزال قومـــه وما يعبدون من دون الله، وحبَّب الله إليه عبادته بعيداً عن أعين قومــه ومــا كانوا عليه من عبادات باطلة، وأوهام زائفة، فكان يـــأخذ طعامــه وشرابــه ويذهب إلى غار حراء كما ثبت في الحديث المتفق عليه أنـــه عليـــه الصــلاة والسلام قال: (جاورت بحراء شهراً...) وحراء هو غار صغير في جبل النــور على بعد ميلين من مكة، فكان يقيم فيه الأيام والليالي ذوات العدد، يقضـــي وقته في عبادة ربه والتفكُّر فيما حوله من مشاهد الكون، وهو غير مطمئن لما عليه قومه من عقائد الشرك الباطلة، والتصورات الواهية، ولكن ليس بين يديه طريق واضح ولا منهج محدد يطمئن إليه و يرضاه.

Chapter Fourteen

حُرُوفُ الجَرِّ

Prepositions

We said that the prepositions or حُرُوفُ الجَرِّ are seventeen in number, we also said that they appear before nouns only. Here we will show how they are all used in sentences and how they affect the nouns that appear after them. The noun and the preposition together are called الجَارُّ و المَجْرُورُ .

The following examples show some of the contextual usages of the prepositions in the order of those most frequently used.

مِنْ : أَعُوذُ بِاللهِ مِنِ الشيطانِ الرَّجيمِ

إِلَى : ذهبتُ إلى المسجدِ

عَلَى : طَلَبُ العِلمِ فَرِيضَةٌ عَلَى كلِّ مسلمٍ و مسلمةٍ

فِي : قال اللهُ تَعَالَى فِي القُرآنِ

عَنْ : سَأَلتُه عَنْ سَبَبِ غِيَابِهِ

بِ : آمَنْتُ بِاللهِ ومَلَائِكَتِهِ

لِ : الحمدُ للهِ عَلَى كلِّ حَالٍ

كَ : الدَّالُ عَلَى الخَيرِ كَفَاعِلِهِ

وَ : واللهِ لَا أَكْذِبُ

تَ : تَاللهِ لَأَكِيدَنَّ أَصْنَامَكُمْ

رُبَّ : رُبَّ صَائِمٍ لَيْسَ لَهُ مِنْ صِيَامِهِ إِلاَّ الجُوعِ

حَتَّى : حَتَّى مَطْلَعِ الفَجْرِ

مُذْ : مَا رَأَيْتُك مُذْ أُسْبُوعٍ

مُنْذُ : ما رأيتكِ مُنْذُ شَهْرٍ

عَدَا : نَجَحَ الطُّلابُ عَدَا زيدٍ

خَلاَ : نَجَحَ الطُّلاَبُ خَلاَ زَيْدٍ

حَاشَا : نَجح الطُّلابُ حَاشَا زيدٍ

The procedure when analysing sentences containing prepositions is as follows:

The children are playing in the playground يَلْعَبُ الأَوْلاَدُ فِي المَلْعَبِ

يلعب : فعل مضارع مرفوع

الأولاد : فاعل مرفوع , الفعل و الفاعل= الجملة الفعلية

في : حرف الجر مبني على السكون

الملعب : اسم مجرور , و الجار و المجرور متعلق بالفعل.

Modesty is part of faith الحَيَاءُ شُعْبَةٌ مِنَ الإِيمَان

الحياء : مبتدأ مرفوع

شعبة : خبر مرفوع , المبتدأ و الخبر= الجملة الاسمية

من : حرف الجر مبني على السكون

الايمان : اسم مجرور , و الجار و المجرور متعلق بالخبر

Salvation is in honesty النَّجَاةُ فِي الصِّدْق

النجاة : مبتدأ مرفوع

في : حرف الجر مبني على السكون

111

الصدق : اسم مجرور, و الجار و المجرور شبه جملة في محل الرفع، خبر،

المبتدأ و الخبر =الجملة الاسمية

لِلْمَسْجِدِ مَنَارَتَان

اللام : حرف الجر مبني على الكسرة

المسجد : اسم مجرور باللام , الجار و المجرور شبه الجملة في محل الرفع،
خبر مقدّم

منارتان : مبتدأ مؤخر مرفوع , المبتدأ و الخبر= جملة اسمية

EXERCISE FOURTEEN

1. Vocalise and translate the following sentences:

- يقطع النجار الخشب بالمنشار

- رأيت الطائر في القفص

- للبستان بابان و على كل باب حارس

– يقطع القطار المسافة من القاهرة إلى الإسكندرية في ثلاث ساعات و عشرين دقيقة

- امتنع المريض عن الأكل و أصبح لا يقوى على المشي

2. Translate the following passage into English and identify all
the حُرُوفُ الجَرِّ:

كان أصحابُ رسولِ الله صلى الله عليه وسلم يحرصون على فـهم دينـهم
ويعملون بتعاليمه السامية وآدابه العالية، فهذا سفيان بن عبد اللّـه يـأتي إلى
رسول اللّه صلى الله عليه وآله وسلم ويقول له. يا رسول اللّه: قل لي في دين
اللّه وشريعته قولاً جامعاً لأصول الدين وفروعه، واضحاً في نفسـه، فـلا
أحتاج بعد سماعي له إلى سؤال غيرك في معرفة الدين، فألزم العمل بمقتضاه،
حتى أفوز برضا اللّه والجنة، فأرشده الرسول صلى الله عليه وآلـه وسـلم إلى
بغيته التي يطلبها. وضالته التي ينشدها، وقال له: "قل آمنـت باللّـه ثم

112

استقم". وهو توجيه نبوي كريم، وإرشاد عظيـــم، وإجابــة وافيــة جمعت الحسنيين، وكلت الاعتقاد والعمل اللذين لابد منهما في الإسلام.

3- Vocalise the following passage paying attention to the words appearing after the prepositions:

وُلِدَ النبي صلى الله عليه وآله وسلَّم في يوم الإثنين الثاني من شهر ربيع الأول الموافق عام خمسمائة وإحدى وسبعين من الميلاد تقريباً، وهو عام الفيل الــذي نصر الله فيه أهل مكة على أبرهة وجيشه وحفظ الله مكة وبيتــها الحــرام، وكان مولده عليه الصلاة والسلام بمكة المكرمة، وكانت أُمّه تحدث أَنها لم تجد حين حطت به ما تجده الحوامل من ثقل ولا وحم ولا غير ذلك. ولمّا ولدتــه أُمّه عليه الصلاة والسلام أرسلت إلى جده، وكان يطوف بالبيت، فجاء إليها فقالت له: يا أبا الحارث وُلِدَ لك غلام عجيب، وأخرجته إليه فأخذه ودخل به الكعبة وعوَّذه ودعا له، ثُمَّ أعاده إلى أُمّه، وهو الذي سمَّاه محمداً وقـــال: إني لأرجو أن يحمده أهل الأرض جميعاً.

4. Analyse the following sentences:

1- يَذْهَبُ حَامِدٌ إِلَى السُّوقِ   2 - الأُسْتَاذَةُ فِي الفَصْلِ

3- لِلرِّجَالِ نَصِيبٌ مِمَّا اكْتَسَبُوا

Chapter Fifteen

حروفُ النَّصبِ

Subjunctive Particles

The subjunctive Particles or حُرُوفُ النَّصْبِ are ten in number. Four of these are used before the فِعْلٌ مُضَارِعٌ, and they are called النَّواصِبُ . The remaining six are used before nouns and are they are called الحُرُوفُ المُشبَّهَةُ بالفِعْلِ or *the particles resembling the verb*. The noun or verb appearing after any of these particles will be مَنْصُوبٌ (accusative) e.g.

الحُرُوفُ المُشبَّهَةُ بالفِعْلِ	النَّواصِبُ
إنَّ اللهَ عَلَى كُلِّ شَيءٍ قَدِيرٌ.	أريدُ أنْ أتعلَّمَ العربية
أعْلَمُ أنَّ اللهَ عَلَى كُلِّ شَيءٍ قَديرٌ	لَنْ يفوزَ الكسول
البَيْتُ جَديدٌ لكِنَّ الأثاثَ قديمٌ	إلْتَحَقْتُ بالمَعهَدِكَي أتَعلَّمَ العَرَبيَّةَ
كأنَّ العِلمَ نُورٌ	سأجتَهِدُ فِي دُروسِي . إذَنْ تَنْجَحَ
لَعَلَّ المَريضَ نَائِمٌ	لَيْتَ الشَّمْسَ طَالِعَةٌ

The أخَوَاتُ إنَّ are also commonly known as الحُرُوفُ المُشَبَّهَةُ بِالفِعْلِ "the sisters of إنَّ ". They introduce a nominal sentence (الجملة) or الاسميــة). The subject (مبتدأ) will then be referred to as إسمُ إنَّ or the noun of إنَّ , in cases where the subject is preceded by إنَّ. In cases where the subject comes after any other of the sisters of إنَّ, then subject will be referred to as the noun of that "sister". The predicate will be مَرُفُوعٌ and is referred to as خَبَرُ إِنَّ or "the predicate of إِنَّ" (and when appearing after any of the sisters of إِنَّ it will be named the predicate of that "sister") e.g.

إِنَّ الكِتَابَ مُفِيْدٌ   (الكتابُ مفيد)

إنَّ: حرف مشبهة بالفعل ، مبني على الفتحة

الكتاب : اسم إنَّ منصوب

مفيدٌ : خبر إن مرفوع . اسم إنَّ و خبرها= الجملة الاسمية

The particle إِنَّ is also called حَرْفُ التَّــأْكِيْدِ or the particle of emphasis. It is used as a means of emphasising the meaning of the sentence and affirming the speech of expression in which it is used. It may introduce a new sentence unlike أَنَّ which cannot be used to introduce a new sentence or idea, instead أَنَّ serves as a conjunction between a nominal and verbal sentence. e.g.

أَنْتَ تَعْلَمُ أَنَّ الإِسْلاَمَ دِينٌ و عَقِيدَةٌ

However إِنَّ may be used after the verb قَالَ even if it appears within the sentence. The particle أَنَّ is not used in such instances e.g.

قَالَ الأُسْتَاذُ إِنَّ الإِمْتِحَانَ قَرِيْبٌ ((و يَقُولُونَ إِنَّه لَمَجْنُون)) ((قُل إِنَّ الأَوَّلِينَ و الآخِرِينَ ...))

The particle أَنَّ is mostly used after the verbs شَهِدَ , عَلِمَ and أَخْبَرَ and their derivatives e.g.

والله يَعْلَمُ أَنَّ المُنَافِقِينَ لَكَاذُبُونَ

And God knows that the hypocrites are liars.

أَشْهَدُ أَنَّ مُحَمَّداً رَسُولُ اللهِ   I bear testimony that Muhammad is the messenger of God.

أَخْبَرَنِي زيدٌ أَنَّه مُسَافِرٌ   Zaid informed me that he is travelling.

The predicate of إِنَّ is often strengthened by a prefixed لَ. This لُ is called لاَمُ التَّأْكِيدِ e.g.

إِنَّ زَيْداً عَالِمٌ   إِنَّ زَيْداً لَعَالِمٌ   ((إِنَّ الإِنْسَانَ لَفِي خُسْرٍ))

The predicate of إِنَّ can, in some cases, appears before the noun of إِنَّ, in such cases the لاَمُ التَّأْكِيدِ is prefixed to the noun e.g.

إِنَّ فِي ذَلِكَ لَعِبْرَةً لِلنَّاسِ   Indeed there is a lesson in that for the people.

إِنَّ فِي البَيَانِ لَسحْراً   Indeed there is magic in speech.

Like إِنَّ and its sisters, the particle لاَ also introduces a nominal sentence. This لاَ is called لاَ النَّافِيَةُ لِلْجِنْسِ or "the لاَ which negates the whole genus." It is regarded as one of the sisters of إِنَّ but it has certain usages e.g.

لاَ رَجُلَ أشجعَ مِنْ زيدٍ   There is no man more brave than Zaid.

لاَ إِلَهَ إِلاَّ اللهُ   There is non worthy of worship but God

لاَ يومَ شِدَّةٍ أهمُّ مِنْ يَومِ الهِجْرَةِ   There is no day more severe than the day of Hijra.

The noun following the لاَ must be نَكِرَةٌ and will not have the nunation, it may be مُفْرَدٌ (not مُضَافٌ), or مُضَافٌ to another

116

noun. It is regarded مُضَافٌ when مَنْصُوبٌ and مُفْرَدٌ when مَبْنِيّ e.g.

لا رجلَ أشجعَ مِنْ زيدٍ

رجُلَ: إسمُ لا مَبْنِيّ عَلَى الفتْحَةِ

لاحَافِظَ القُرآنِ فِي هَذِهِ القَرْيَةِ

حَافِظَ: إسمُ لا مَنْصُوبٌ

The predicate of لا must be nominative (مَرْفُوعٌ). The predicate is in some cases expressed while in others it is omitted (مَحْذُوفٌ) e.g.

There is no in our street more beautiful than this one.	لا بيتَ فِي شَارعِنَا أجملُ مِنْ هَذَا البَيْتِ
There no any book on the table.	لا كِتَابَ عَلَى المَائِدَة
I do not have any money.	لا مَالَ عِنْدِي
There is none worthy of worship but God.	لا الَهِ (موجودٌ) إلا الله
There is no power nor mighty except with God.	لا حولَ (موجودٌ) و لا قوةَ (موجودة) إلاَّ بِاللَّهِ

In order for the لا to have a governing force over the noun following it, it is a condition that the noun of لا be نكرة and appear before the predicate. If the subject following لا is معرفة or if it precedes لا, this لا losses its governing force and must be repeated e.g.

لا مُحَمَّدٌ فِي الحُجْرَةِ و لا مَحْمُودٌ   لا فِي الفَصْلِ تِلْمِيذٌ و لاَ تِلْمِيذَةٌ

When denying the presence or existence of two things using لا,
the following end cases will be valid

١) لا كتابَ و لا جريدةَ على المائدة

٢) لا كتابَ و لا جريدةً على المائدة

٣) لا كتابَ و لا جريدةٌ على المائدة

٤) لا كتابٌ و لا جريدةٌ على المائدة

٥) لا كتابٌ و لا جريدةَ على المائدة

IMPORTANT TERMS

النواصب (1	The accusative agents	
الحروف المشبهة بالفعل (2	The particles resembling the verb	
أخوات إنَّ (3	The sisters of إنّ	
اسم إنَّ (4	The noun of إنّ	
خبر إنَّ (5	The predicate of إنَّ	
لا النافية للجنس (6	The لا which negates the whole genus	

EXERCISE FIFTEEN

1) Vocalise the following sentences:

ان الدرس سهل لكنّ الطالب كسلان

أخبرني إبراهيم ان سليم لم يحضر لأنه مريض لكن فاطمة حضرت.

ان هذا الكتاب لا ريب فيه وهو يهدينا إلى الحق.

لا شكّ ان القمر كبير لكن الأرض أكبر.

يا أحمد ماذا قلت لمحمد لما طلب منك الكتاب و الجريدة ؟ أنا قلت له انه
لا كتاب و لا جريدة عندي.

118

لا عندي كتاب و لا جريدة و لذلك لا أقرأ شيء اليوم.

ان لكل أمة فتنة و فتنة أمتي المال.

ليت المسلم يقتدي بالنبي.

ان الطيور على أشكالها تقع.

2) Fill in the blanks with a suitable subjunctive particle:

1) الحصان سريع ... الفهد أسرع   2)سمعتُ. ..زيدا قادم من الحج

3)...... الباطل كان زهوقا   4).......... النظافة واجبة

5) يسّرني .... النتيجة حسنة   6) يؤلمني ..... البنت مريضة

7)........المنزل قريب   8) أخبرَني يوسف....عمر رجع

3) Begin each of the following sentences with إنَّ :

1) الحقيبتان صغيرتان   2) لمهندسون ماهرون.

3) التلميذان مجتهدان   4)باب الحديقة مفتوح

5) المؤمنات صالحات

4) Analyse the following sentences:

1) الحديقة جميلة لكن البستاني كسلان   2) علم المدرس أن الطالب غائب

3) كأن العلم نور   4) إن الأخلاق الحسنة تدخلك الجنة

5) لعل الدرس سهل   6) ليت العطلة قريبة

Chapter Sixteen

النَّوَاصِبُ

The Accusative Agents

The accusative agents or النَّوَاصِبُ are the four particles used before a verb. They are causative and govern the present tense verb (المضارع) making it مَنْصُوبٌ.

The particle أنْ called حَرْفٌ مَصْدَرِيَّةٌ (lit. the verbal noun particle). When this particle is used together with a verb it replaces the مَصْدَرٌ (verbal noun) e.g.

أريدُ أن أخرجَ – أريدُ الخروجَ I want to come out.

أرْجُو أنْ تنجحَ – أرجُو نَجَاحَكَ I hope you will succeed.

It may be translated as " to " or "that " e.g.

I require you to open this door. أطلبُ مِنْكَ أنْ تفتحَ هذا البابَ.

I am unable to carry this chair. لا أقدرُ أنْ أحْمِلَ هذا الكرسيَّ.

I hope that he returns today. أرجُو أنْ يرجعَ اليَوْمَ.

I hope that you do not go today. أرْجُو ألّا تَذْهَبَ اليَوْمَ (أن + لا=ألّا)

The particle لَنْ is used for negation, and is known as حَرْفُ النَّفْي. It negates the occurrence of an action in the future e.g.

I know that you will never come back to us. أنَا أعْرِفُ أنَّك لَنْ تَرْجِعَ إلينَا

I will never lie. لَنْ أكْذِبَ

The particle كَي is used with the present tense verb to express the purpose behind the action e.g.

I go to the institute in order to learn.	كَي أَتَعَلَّمَ أَذهَبُ إلى المَعْهَدِ
I study so that I may serve society.	لِكَي أَخدِمَ المُجْتَمَعَ أَدْرُسُ
I work hard in my studies so that I do not fail.	كَيْلاَ أَجتَهِدُ في دُرُوسِي أَرْسبَ

The particle إذَنْ is used in reply to a statement previously made e.g.

I shall work hard in the exam. In that case you will pass.	سَأَجتَهِدُ في الامتِحانِ إذَنْ تَنْجَحَ.
I shall be trustworthy.	سَأَكُونُ أَمِيناً
Then your business will be profitable.	إذَنْ تَرَبَحَ تِجَارُتُكَ

The above-mentioned particles are the basic subjunctive particles that govern a verb. Apart from these there are five other particles that also render the verb منصوب , these are called حُرُوفُ النَّصْبِ الفَرْعِيَّـةُ or the secondary subjunctive particles. These are five in number and they are:

لام التَّعْلِيلِ (لـ:)

دَخَلْتُ المَعْهَدَ لأَتَعَلَّمَ .   فَتَحْتُ النَّافِذَةَ لِيَدْخُلَ الهَوَاءَ

لام الجُحُود (لـ):

مَا كَانَ الصَّدِيقُ لِيَخُونَ صَدِيقَةُ.   لَمْ يَكُنِ المُسلِمُ لِيَكْذِبَ

فاء السَّبَبِيَّةِ (فَ):

إجتَهِدْ في الدَّرسِ فَتَفُوزَ في الامتِحَانِ.   لَمْ يُسأَلْ فَيَجِيبَ

حَتَّى:

إجتَهِدْ حَتَّى تَنْجَحَ .   لاَ تَدْخُلْ حَتَّى يُؤذَنَ لَكَ

واو اْلَمَعِيَّةِ (و):

لا تَأْكُلْ وَتَقْرَأَ . لَمْ يَفْعَلْ الخَيْرَ وَيَنْدَمَ . لا تَأْمُرْ بِالصِّدْقِ وَتَكْذِبَ

The لام التَّعْلِيْل or " The ل of cause " is used with the verb to show the purpose of the action and resembles the particle كي e.g.

I shook the tree so that its fruits would fall.   هَزَزْتُ الشَّجَرَةَ لِيَسْقُطَ ثَمَرَهَا

I shook the tree so its fruits would fall   هَزَزْتُ الشَّجَرَةَ كَي يَسْقُطَ ثَمَرَهَا

I shook the tree in order for its fruits to fall   هَزَزْتُ الشَّجَرَةَ لِكَيْ يَسْقُطَ ثَمَرَهَا

The لام الجُحُود or " the ل of denial " is used after the verb كَانَ in the negative e.g.

God will not help the oppressors.   مَا كَانَ اللهُ لِيَنْصُرَ الظَّالِمِينَ

A Muslin should not ignore his brother.   لَمْ يَكُنْ المُسْلِمُ لِيَهْجُرَ أَخَاهُ

The article فَـاء السَّـبَبِيَّةِ or " the فَ of reason " follows a negative statement or command in the positive or negative e.g.

He did not work hard in order to pass.   لَمْ يَجْتَهِدْ فَيَنْجَحَ (نفي)

Work hard in order to pass.   إِجْتَهِدْ فَتَنْجَحَ (أمر)

Don't be lazy because you may fail.   لا تَكْسَلْ فَتَرْسَبَ (نهي)

The particle حتى has the same meaning as the لام التعليل, it also has another purpose and meaning; to show finality e.g.

Do good so that you may enter paradise.   إعْمَلُ الخَيْرَ حَتى تَدْخُلَ الجَنَّةَ

I came so that I could acquire knowledge.   جِئْتُ إلى المَدْرَسَةِ حَتى أَنَالَ العِلْمَ

I shall wait until he returns.   سَأَنْتَظِرُ حَتَى يَرْجِعَ

Fast until the sun sets.   صُمْ حَتَى تَغِيبَ الشَّمْسَ

The وَاو ألْمَعِيَّـــةِ like the فَاء السَّـــبَبِيَّةِ also follows a negative statement or a negative command e.g

Do not eat fish and (with it) drink milk.   لا تَأكُلْ السَّمَكَ و تَشْرَبَ اللَّبَنَ

Do not prohibit bad characteristics whilst you do the same.   لا تَنْهَ عَنْ خُلْقٍ و تَأتِيَ مِثْلَهُ

SUMMARY

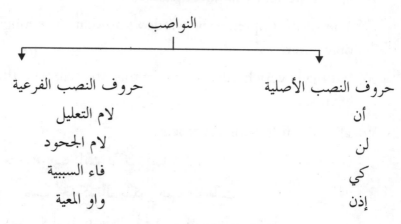

حروف النصب الفرعية	النواصب	حروف النصب الأصلية
لام التعليل		أن
لام الجحود		لن
فاء السببية		كي
واو المعية		إذن

IMPORTANT TERMS

1) حروف النصب الأصلية   The primary Subjunctive Particles

2) حروف النصب الفرعية   The secondary subjunctive particles

3) لام التعليل   The ل of cause

4) لام الجحود   The ل of denial

5) فاء السببية   The فَ of reason

EXERCISE SIXTEEN

1) Translate the following sentences:

   a) Ahmad came in order to go with you to the mosque.

   b) Salim is reading in poor/weak light. In that case his eyesight will become weak.

   c) My sister said that she will never stay absent from school.

   d) Salma loves to read and Hamid loves to write.

   e) We love to eat fish and the boys love to eat chicken.

   f) A lazy student will never pass.

   g) The servant opened the windows so that the sunlight may enter.

   h) Fatima is very hardworking. In that she will pass the exams.

2) Vocalise the following sentences:

   a) فتحت باب المسجد كي أصلّي الفجر

   b) أن يحبّ أحدكم أن يأكل لحم أخيه الميّت

   c) (هو) كباسط يديه إلَى فيه ليبلغ فاه وما هو ببالغه

   d) لا تنظر إلى عيوب الناس و تهمل عيوب نفسك

   e) لا تأكل كثيراً فتمرض

3) Translate the following passage into English and identify all the accusative agents:

أراد الله سبحانه وتعالى أن يُري للرسول صلّى الله عليه وسلّم بعض آياتــــه، لِيُسَرّى عنه بعد وفاة زوجته السيدة خديجة رضي الله عنها، وعمّه أبي طالب،

وبعد أن عاد صلَّى الله عليه وآله وسلَّم من رحلة الطائف، وقد خذله أهلها.

في هذه الفترة الحرجة أنعمه الله تعالى بالإسراء والمعراج ليثبّته وليعينه علـــى مقاومة كفار مكـــة، و لكي يكرمه في أعقاب سنين طويلـــة مـــن العمـــل والصمود من أجل الدعوة الإسلامية. أُسْري بالرسول صلَّى الله عليه وسلَّم ليلاً من المسجد الحرام بمكة المكرَّمة إلى المسجد الأقصى ببيت المقدس، راكباً على البراق، وكان معه جبريل عليه السلام، فنزل هناك وصلَّى بالأنبياء إماماً، ثُمَّ عُرِجَ به صلَّى الله عليه وسلَّم إلى السماء، حيث فرض الله عليه وعلى أمته الصلاة خمس مرات في اليوم والليلة.

Chapter Seventeen

حروفُ الجَزْمِ

The Jussive Particles

The jussive particles or حُرُوفُ الجَزْمِ are five in number. These appear before the فِعْلٌ مُضَارِعٌ and effect the end-case causing the verb to be مَجْزُومٌ (jussive) which is shown by a *sukun* (anti-vowel) over the final radical. The jussive end-case is shown by the omission of the final ن in the case of the five verbs (الأفْعالُ الخَمْسَةُ). The following are what grammar scholars call the *five verbs*:

a) Two present tense verbs with the added letter ألف (*alif*) to denote the masculine or feminine dual e.g.

يَذْهَبَانِ

They are going. (dual masc.)

تَذْهَبَانِ

You are going. (dual masc. & fem.) - They are going. (dual. fem)

b) Two present tense verbs with the added letter و (*waw*) denoting the masculine plural e.g.

يَذْهَبُونَ

They are going. (plural masc.)

تَذْهَبُوْنَ

You are going. (plural masc.)

c) The verb with the letter ي denoting the feminine second person e.g.

تَذْهَبِيْنَ

You are going. (sing. fem.)

The five verbs retain the final ن when they are in the nominative form (مَرْفُوعٌ) e.g.

The two friends are travelling tomorrow.	الصَّدِيقَانِ يُسَافِرَانِ غَدَاً
You are travelling tomorrow. (dual)	أَنْتُمَا تُسَافِرَانِ غَدَاً
The Muslims fast in the month of Ramadan	المُسْلِمُونَ يَصُومُونَ فِي شَهْرِ رَمَضَان
Do you know the meaning of this word? (fem.)	هَلْ تَعْرِفِينَ مَعْنَى هَذِهِ الكَلِمَةِ؟

However, when they are in the accusative and jussive form the final ن will be dropped e.g.

It gives me pleasure when you memorise your lessons.	يُسْعِدِنِي أَنْ تَحْفَظُوا دُرُوسَكُمْ
Zaid and Ibrahim refused to go to America.	رَفَضَ زَيْدٌ و إِبْرَاهِيْمُ أَنْ يَذْهَبَا إِلَى أَمْرِيْكَا
O Fatimah! Why didn't you write the lesson?	لِمَذَا لَمْ تَكْتُبِي الدَّرْسَ يَا فَاطِمَةُ؟

The jussive particles (حُرُوفُ الجَزْمِ) are:

I did not leave the house today.	لَمْ : لم يخرجْ من المنزل اليوم
Khalid has not gone out from the house yet.	لَمَّا : لَمَّا يخرجْ خالد من المنزل بعد
Khalid should go out from the house.	لِ : ليخرجْ خالد من المنزل
Do not go out in the cold weather.	لاَ : لا تخرجْ في الجوّ البارد

If you go out in the cold weather you will be sick.

إنْ : إنْ تخرجْ في الجوّ البارد تمرض

When the particle لَمْ appears before a present tense verb it converts the meaning to past tense, and in such cases its meaning will be like the مَا of negation that appears before a past tense verb e.g.

مَا كتبتُ الدرسَ I did not write the lesson. لَمْ أكتبْ الدرسَ

مَا قرأنا الجريدةَ We did not read the لَمْ نقرأْ الجريدةَ اليومَ
اليوم newspaper today.

The particle لَمَّـا conveys the sense of the negative past tense equal to "not yet" e.g.

Zaid has not yet present. لَمَّا يحْضُرْ زَيْدٌ

I have not yet completed my studies. لَمَّا أُكْمِلْ الدِّرَاسَةَ

The particle لـ converts the meaning to the imperative and is called لام الأمـر or the imperative *lam*. It is prefixed to the present tense verb for the third person and expresses the meaning of a command e.g.

Khalid should go out from the class. ليخرجْ خالد من الفصل

Zainab should be present in the lesson. لتحضرْ زينب في الدرس

Man should look at what he was فلينظرْ الإنسان مما خُلِقَ
created from.

The student should go out calmly. و ليخرجْ الطلاب بهدوء

The particle لا is called لا النَّاهِية or the prohibitive لا, it denotes the prohibition of an act conveyed by the verb it introduces, or a wish that something should not be done. It is the opposite of the imperative e.g.

Do not laugh a lot.   لا تكثرْ من الضحك

Do not open this door, O boys!   لا تفتحُوا هذا الباب يا أولاد

The particle إنْ is called إن شَرْطِية or the conditional إنْ. Unlike the above mentioned particles which govern only one verb, إن شَرْطِية governs two verbs. The first verb is called فِعلُ الشَّرْطِ and the second is called فِعْلُ الجَوَاب and according to some scholars, جَوَابُ الشَّرطِ e.g.

If you help me I will help you.   إنْ تنصرْني أنصرْك

If you are hasty you will regret.   إنْ تعجلْ تندمْ

IMPORTANT TERMS

1) حروف الجزم   The jussive particles.

2) لام الأمر   The imperative لـ.

3) لا الناهية   The prohibitive لـ.

4) إنْ الشرطية   The conditional إنْ.

EXERCISE SEVENTEEN

1) Vocalise the following:

2) ان تنصروا الله ينصركم   1) لا تخافي و لا تحزني

4) لما يثمر بستاننا   2) قال لا تخافا إنني معكما أسمع و أري

6) لم تمطر السماء اليوم   5) لينفق كل واحد من ماله

8) لم يحضر زيد البارحة   7) إن تجتهد تنجح

10) ليجلس كل طالب في مكانة   9) لا تأكل و أنت شبعان

129

2) Fill in the blanks with a suitable jussive particle:

١) ......تقرب من النار تشعر بحرارتها

٢) الفلاح ....يحلب بقرته

٣) .... تسرع في السير

٤) .... يذهب زيد إلى السوق

٥) .... يحفظ كل طالبة درسها

٦) .... يسافر أخوك تسافر معه

3) Analyse the following sentences:

لا تكثر من الضحك (2   إن تجتهد تنجح (1

لينفق كل واحد من ماله (3

4) Translate the following passage into English:

كان عبد الله والد الرسول عليه الصلاة والسلام هو أصغر أبناء عبد المطلـــب وأحبهم إلى قلبه، فلما أصبح شاباً فتياً ذهب به والده عبد المطلب يريد تزويجه حتى أتى به إلى وهب بن عبد مناف بن زهرة سيد قومه فزوّجه ابنته آمنـــة بنـــت وهب، وهي يومئذٍ أفضل امرأة في قريش نسباً وموضعاً. وبعد زواج عبـــد الله بن عبد المطلب من آمنة بقليل، خرج من مكة قاصداً الشام في تجـــارة وتـــرك زوجته وهي حامل بالرسول عليه الصلاة والسلام، وعند عودته من الشام نزل بالمدينة عند أخواله بني النجار فأقام عندهم شهراً وهو مريض وتوفي ودُفِـــنَ في يثرب وله من العمر حوالي خمس وعشرون عاماً، ولم يترك عبد الله لزوجتـــه سوى جاريته أُم أيمن بركة الحبشية، وخمسة جمال، وبعضاً من الغنم.

Chapter Eighteen

غَيْرُ العَامِلَةِ الحُرُوفُ

The Non-Causative Particles

The we call الحُرُوفُ غَيْرُ العَامِلَةِ or non-causative particles are those particles which do not govern the words appearing after them. i.e. they do not cause a change to the end-case of the words that follow them. These particles can be divided into the following groups:

1) حُرُوفُ الجَوَابِ -The particles of affirmation. These particles are the particles used to reply a question and they are:

(i). نَعَمْ : Meaning "yes", and used to verify a positive or negative question e.g.

Did I not tell you that I would pass? Yes, you told me.	أَلَم أَقُلْ لَكَ إِنِّي سَأَنْجَحُ؟ نَعَمْ قُلْتَ لِي
Is this a primary school? Yes.	أَهَذِه مَدْرَسَةٌ ابْتِدَائِيَّةٌ؟ نَعَمْ

(ii). أَجَــلْ : "Yes", similar to the above (نعم), and also used to confirm a statement e.g.

The rain is falling. "Yes!"	يَنْزِلُ المَطَرُ. أَجَلْ

(iii). بَلَى : "Yes indeed" , "of course", "certainly". It is used to reply a negative question in the affirmative e.g.

Am I not your Lord? Of course (you are)!	أَلَسْتُ بِرِّبِّكُمْ؟ بَلَى!

(iv). لَا : "No", used to reply in the negative e.g.

Do you speak Japanese? No, I do not speak Japanese.	هَلْ تَتَكَلَّمُ اللُّغَةَ اليَابَانِيَّةَ؟ لَا لَا أَتكَلَّمُ اليَابَانِيَّةَ

(2) حُرُوفُ الاسْتِفْهَامِ the interrogative particles: The interrogative particles are used when asking a question. There are two interrogative particles and they are:

(i) هَلْ : Meaning "is", "are". This particle is used to introduce a positive question. The reply may be positive or negative e.g.

هَلْ يَذْهَبُ زَيْدٌ إِلَى المَدِينَة؟   Is Zaid going to Madina?

هَلْ أَنْتَ مِنْ جُنُوبِ أَفْرِيقِيَا؟   Are you from South Africa?

The letter أ, which when used as an interrogative is translated as "is?" "are?" is used to introduce a positive or negative question. It is mostly used when confirming one of two things e.g.

أ ذَهَبْتَ إِلَى الجامعة؟

نعم ذَهَبْتُ إِلَى الجامعة / لا ما ذهبتُ إِلَى الجامعة

أَلَمْ أَقُل لَّكَ إِنَّ زَيداً رَاجِعٌ اليومَ؟

بَلَى ، (قُلتَ) / نَعَمْ (لَمْ تَقُلْ شَيئاً)

أهذه مدرسةٌ ثانويّةٌ أم ابتِدائيّةٌ؟

NOTE : Apart from the above two words used for questioning, there are other words which are not particles but nouns. These are called أَسْمَاءُ الاسْتِفْهَامِ or the *interrogative nouns* e.g.

أيّ   مَتَي   أَيْنَ   كَيْفَ   مَنْ   مَا

IMPORTANT TERMS

1) حروف الجواب   The particles of Affirmation.

2) حروف الاستفهام   The Particles of Interrogation

3) أسماء الاستفهام   The interrogative nouns

132

EXERCISE EIGHTEEN

1) Translate the following into English:

عَنْ أبي هُرَيْرَةَ رَضِيَ اللّٰه عَنْهُ قال: أَتَى النَّبِيَّ صَلَّى اللّٰه عليهِ وآلهِ وَسلَّمَ رَجُـلٌ
أَعْمَى،- فَقَالَ: يا رَسُولَ اللّٰه! لَيْسَ لي قَائِدٌ يَقُودُني إلى المسجدِ. فَسَأل رَسُولَ
اللّٰه صلى الله عليه وآله وسلم أَنْ يُرَخِّص لَهُ أَنْ يُصَلِّي في بَيْتِهِ. فَرَخَّصَ لَـهُ.
فَلَمَّا وَلَّى دَعَاهُ فَقَالَ: "هَلْ تَسْمَعُ النِّدَاءَ؟". قال: نَعَم. قال: "فَـأجِبْ-"رواه
مسلم

Chapter Nineteen

حروفُ العَطفِ

The Conjunctions

Letters that link words and sentences are called حُرُوفُ العَطفِ or conjunctions. The words or sentences appearing before the conjunction is called مَعْطُوفٌ عليهِ and the word or sentence appearing after the conjunction is called the مَعْطُوفٌ. The مَعْطُوفٌ will follow the مَعْطُوفٌ عليهِ in its end –case e.g.

ذَهَبَ زَيْدٌ وَ خَالِدٌ   Zaid and Khalid went.

ذهب : فعل ماضي مبني علي الفتحة

زيد : فاعل مرفوع و معطوف عليه

و : حرف العطف مبني على الفتحة

خالد : معطوف مرفوع

The conjunctions used in Arabic are as follows:

i)- و "And" , used to join the two single nouns or sentences e.g.

نَضَجَ الخُوخُ و العِنَبُ (مفرد)

إنْ تَرعَدِ السّماء وتبرقْ فلا تخرجْ مِن البيتِ (الجملة)

أكَلَتُ الخوخَ و العنبَ (مفرد)

يَخَافُ الأطْفَالُ مِنْ أنْ تَرعدَ السّماءُ و تبرقَ (الجملة)

هذا دكّانُ الفَوَاكِهِ والثِمَارِ (المفرد)

ترعد السماءُ و تبرقُ (الجملة)

ii) فَ - "Then", "So", the particle فَ is used to show a sequence (تَعْقِيْبٌ) or immediate succession (تَرْتِيْبٌ) e.g.

The teacher entered and then the principal. دَخَلَ المُدَرِّسُ فَالمُدِيْرُ

He washed his face then his hands. غَسَلَ وَجْهَهُ فَيَدَيْه

iii) ثُمَّ - "Then", "thereupon", shows a delayed succession e.g.

Abu Bakr died followed by Umar. مَاتَ أَبُو بَكر ثُمَّ عُمَرُ

iv) أَو - "Or", implies a sense of choice (خِيَارٌ) or doubt (شَكٌّ) e.g.

Drink the juice or tea. إِشْرَبْ العَصِيْرَ أَوْ الشَّاي (خيار)

The teacher said the exam is on Thursday, or he said, on Friday. قَالَ الأُسْتَاذُ إِنَّ الامتحانَ يَوْمَ الخَمِيْسِ أَوْ قَالَ يَوْمَ الجُمْعَةِ (شكّ)

v) أَمْ - "Or", used in an interrogative sentence along with the interrogative particle e.g.

Is Khadijah in the faculty of medicine or in the faculty of law? هَلْ خَدِيْجَةٌ فِي كُلِّيَّةِ الطِّبِّ أَمْ كُلِّيَّةِ القَانُون ؟

vi) بَل - "But", "rather", "nay", used to relinquish one notion for another e.g.

Zaid was not present but Khalid. ما حضر زيدٌ بل خالدٌ

I bought an apple, (I mean) an orange. إِشْتَرَيْتُ تُفَاحاً بَلْ بُرْتُقَالاً

vii) لَكِنْ - "But", "however", similar to بَل e.g.

But you thought that God does not know a lot of what you are doing... وَلَكِنْ ظَنَنْتُمْ أَنَّ اللهَ لاَ يَعْلَمُ كَثِيْراً مِمَّا تَعْمَلُون...

viii) لا - "Not", used as a negation. The statement preceding it should be positive or an imperative e.g.

135

Take the book, not the pen. خُذِ الكِتَابَ لاَ القَلَمَ

I ate the apple, not the orange. أَكَلْتُ التُّفَاحَ لاَ البُرْتُقَالَ

ix) حَتَّـــى – "Even" , "including" . This is used as a conjugation for a noun only , the معطوف must be part of the معطوف عليه e.g.

The army fled even the commander. فَرَّ الجَيْشُ حَتَّى القَائِدُ

I ate the orange including the peel. أَكَلْتُ البُرْتُقَالَ حَتَّى قِشْرَه

EXERCISE NINETEEN

1) Vocalise the following sentences:

2) أ مدرس أنت أم طالب   1) بنى الأمير قصر و حصن

4) أكل الفيل الفاكهة حتى قشرها   3) أ أنت فعلت هذا أم زيد

6) ما غرست نخل لكن قمح   5) قدّمت إليه الطعام فأكلة

8) هززت الشجرة فسقط ثمرها   7) ذهب الرئيس لا الوزير

10) نجحت سعاد و أختها في الامتحان .   9) بذر الفلاح الحبّ ثمّ حصده

2) Fill the blanks with a suitable conjunction:

1) اختلف التاجر ......و كيله

2) ما باع الفلاح الشعير .... القمح

3) لبث الضيف عندنا يوما .... بعض يوم

4) رافق الأخيار..... الأشرار

5) أزيد ذهب .... أخوه؟

6) دخل المدير .... المدرسون

7) أراد الطالب أن يفتح الكتاب ...... يقرأه

8) ما قرأت الكتاب كله .... بعضه

9) اقرأ جريدة .... مجلة

10) أكلت السمكة .... رأسه

3) Analyse the following sentences:

1) رأيت الأسد لا النمر

2) خسر التاجر كل شيء حتى شرفه

3) خذ وردا أو بنفسجا

4) Translate the following into English:

عَنْ أَبِي هُرَيْرَةَ رَضِيَ اللّه عَنْهُ قال: قال رَسُولُ اللّه صلى الله عليـــــه وآلــــه وسلم :مَنْ نَسِيَ وهو صائِمٌ فَأَكَلَ أو شَرِبَ فَلْيُتِمَّ صَوْمَهُ، فَإِنَّما أَطْعَمَهُ اللّـــهُ وَسَقَاهُ - متفق عليه

Chapter Twenty

أَسْمَاءُ الاسْتِفْهَامِ
The Interrogative Noun

In chapter eighteen we discussed the interrogative particles under the non-causative particles. In this chapter we will discuss in details the أَسْمَاء الإِسْتِفْهَامِ or the *interrogative nouns*. The interrogative nouns are the nouns used to introduce a question. They are ten in number and always appear as the first word of the sentence, and they are:

كَيْفَ مَتَى مَاذَا مَا مَنْ أَيَّان أَنَّى أَيْنَ

كَمْ أَيُّ

The Interrogative nouns are all indeclinable and are analysed according to their position in the sentence (فِي مَحَلٍّ). Apart from the above mentioned nouns, the particles أ and هَلْ are also used to introduce questions. However, since these two are particles and not nouns they cannot be discussed here. We have already discussed these two under non-causative particles. Moreover, they are unique in the sense that they do not have any grammatical position in a sentence (لا مَحَلَّ لَهَا مِنَ الإِعْرَابِ).

The interrogative مَنْ is used to question about rational (human) beings only (ذَوِ العُقُولِ) e.g.

Who are you?   مَنْ أَنْتَ ؟

Who broke the idols?	مَنْ كَسَرَ الأَصْنَامَ؟
Who is this boy with you?	مَنِ الوَلَدُ الذِي مَعَكِ ؟
Who did this?	مَنْ فَعَلَ هَذَا؟

When مَـنْ is followed by an *indefinite noun* it becomes the subject of the sentence (مبتدأ), and when it is followed by a *definite noun* it is the advanced predicate (خبر مقدّم) e.g.

Who is absent? مَنْ غَائِبٌ ؟

مَنْ : اسم الاستفهام مبني على السكون في محل الرفع <u>مبتدأ</u>

Who are you? مَنْ أَنْتَ ؟

مَنْ : اسم الاستفهام مبني على السكون في محل الرفع خبر <u>مقدم</u>

When مَـن is followed by a verb, من will be the *advanced direct object* if the verb is transitive, and the subject , if the verb is intransitive e.g.

Who did you see? مَنْ رَأَيْتَ ؟

من : اسم الاستفهام مبني على السكون في محل النصب <u>مفعول مقدم</u>.

مَنْ ذَهَبَ إلى السُّوق ؟

من : اسم الأَستفهام مبني على السكون في محل الرفع <u>مبتدأ</u>.

However, if the verb following من is transitive and has a mentioned *direct object,* من will be treated as the *subject,* and the sentence following it will be treated as the *predicate* e.g.

Who wrote the lesson? مَنْ كَتَبَ الدَّرْسَ ؟

من : اسم الاستفهام مبني على السكون في محل الرفع <u>مبتدأ</u>.

كتب الدرس : الجملة الفعلية في محل الرفع <u>خبر</u>

The interrogative مَا and مَاذَا are used when questioning about inanimate objects as well other non-rational animate things such as animals (غَـيْرُ ذَوِ العُقُـول). The procedure when analysing sentences containing these words is the one we used above:

What is this?   مَا هَذَا ؟

ما : اسم الاستفهام مبني على السكون في محل الرفع خبر مقدم.

What do you have?   مَا عِنْدَكَ ؟

ما : اسم الاستفهام مبني على السكون في محل الرفع مبتدأ.

What did you see?   مَاذَا رَأَيْتَ ؟

ماذا : اسم الاستفهام مبني على السكون في محل النصب مفعول مقدم.

NOTE: When مَـــا is prefixed by the حُرُوفِ الجَرِّ the *alif* is omitted e.g.

بِمَ = ب + مَا   لِمَ = ل + مَا   عَمَّ = عَنْ + مَا

فِيمَ = فِي + مَا   مِمَّ = مِنْ + مَا   عَلامَ = عَلَى + مَا

When the letter لِ is prefixed to the word مَاذَا it converts the meaning from "what" to "why" e.g.

Why were you not present
in class today?   لِمَاذَا لَمْ تَحْضُرْ اليومَ فِي الفَصْلِ؟

Why are you laughing?   لِمَذَا تَضْحَكُ؟

The interrogative مَتَـــي and أَيْنَ are used to ask questions relating to time and place respectively (زَمَانٌ و مَكَانٌ) they are adverbs (ظُرُوفٌ) and are thus analysed as مَفْعُولٌ فِيهِ when they are followed by verbs. When followed by nouns they are analysed as an *advanced predicate* e.g.

When did you come to the university?   مَتَى جِئْتَ إِلَى الجَامِعَةِ ؟

مَتَى : اسم الاستفهام مبني على السكون في محل النصب مفعول فيه
(ظرف الزمان)

Where did you go?   أيْنَ ذَهَبْتَ؟

أين : اسم الاستفهام مبني على الفتحة في محل النصب مفعول فيه
(ظرف المكان)

When is the examination?   مَتَى الامْتِحانُ؟

مَتَى : اسم الاستفهام مبني على السكون في محل الرفع خبر مقدم .

Where is the airport?   أيْنَ المَطَارُ؟

أيْنَ : اسم الاستفهام مبني على الفتحة في محل الرفع خبر مقدم

The interrogative كَيْفَ is used to question about the state, circumstance, or condition of things (حَالٌ). If it is followed by a noun it will be treated as an *advanced predicate*, and if followed by a verb it is حَالٌ (*circumstantial*) e.g.

How are you?   كَيْفَ أنْتَ ؟

كيف : اسم الاستفهام مبني على الفتحة في محل الرفع خبر مقدم

How did you go?   كَيْفَ ذَهَبْتَ؟

اسم الاستفهام مبني على الفتحة في محل النصب حال

The word أيَّانَ is also used to ask about time (زَمَانٌ) when something is long over due. However, this word is not commonly used. It is analysed in the same manner as مَتَى e.g.

When are you returning?   أيَّانَ تَعُودُ؟

أيان : اسم الاستفهام مبني على الفتحة في محل النصب مفعول فيه
(ظرف الزمان)

When is the day of judgement?   أيَّانَ يَوْمُ القِيَامَةِ؟

أيان : اسم الاستفهام مبني على الفتحة في محل الرفع خبر مقدم

The interrogative أنَّى is also less common, and it has both an interrogative meaning and a non-interrogative one e.g.

So approach your fields ... ...   فَأْتُوا حَرْثَكُمْ أَنَّى شِئْتُمْ

however you wish......

أنَّى : اسم الاستفهام مبني على السكون في محل النصب حال (ـ كيف)

Where did you get this from?   أنَّى لَكِ هَذَا؟

أنَّى: اسم الاستفهام مبني على السكون في محل الرفع خبر مقدم (أين)

The word أيّ is used to ask questions regarding ذَو العُقُول

and ذَو العُقُول غَيْر, masculine and feminine alike. It is declinable and is analysed as such e.g.

Which student is sick?   أيُّ طَالِبٍ مَرِيْضٌ ؟

أي : مبتدأ مرفوع و مضاف

Which book did you read?   أيُّ كِتَابٍ قَرَأْتَ؟

أي : مفعول مقدم منصوب و مضاف

What are you writing with?   بِأيِّ شَيْءٍ تَكْتُبُ ؟

أي : اسم مجرور بالباء و مضاف

The interrogative كَمْ is used to ask questions regarding numbers (عَـدَدٌ). The noun appearing after كَمْ is called تَمْيِيزٌ (specification) and should be singular and in the *accusative* end-case (مَنْصُوبٌ) e.g.

How many books did you read?   كَمْ كِتَاباً قَرَأْتَ؟

كم : اسم الاستفهام مبني على السكون في محل النصب مفعول مقدم

It (كَمْ) is at times prefixed by the حُرُوفٌ. The noun following it in such a case may be accusative or genitive e.g.

For how much *Rials* did you رِيَالٍ اشْتَرَيْتَ هَذَا الكِتَابَ؟ / رِيَالاً بِكَمْ buy this book?

بكم : الباء حرف الجر مبني على الكسرة

كم : اسم الاستفهام مبني على السكون في محل الجر , الجار و المجـــرور متعلق الفعل اشتريت

The word كَـــمْ is also used to express abundance, and in such cases it will be used to introduce a statement instead of a question. This kind of is called كَمْ الجَارية (the *genitive* كم). The noun following this كم should be *genitive*(مجرور) , it may be singular or plural e.g.

So many a book I have read! كم كتابٍ قرأتُ!

So many books I have read! كم كتبٍ قرأتُ!

The تَمْيِيزٌ of كم الاستفهام is at times omitted, in such cases it will be treated as the predicate brought forward. When كم الاستفهام is followed by an *intransitive verb* it will be treated as the subject e.g.

كَمْ عُمرُكَ ؟ كم (سنةً) عُمرُكَ؟

كَمْ أَوْلاَدُكَ ؟ كم (ولداً) أولادُك ؟

كم : اسم الاستفهام مبني على السكون في محل الرفع خبر مقدم.

عمرك: مبتدأ مؤخر مرفوع و مضاف , و تمييز كم محذوف تقديره كم "سنة" عمرك ؟

كَمْ طَالِباً جَاءَ ؟

كم : اسم الاستفهام مبني على السكون في محل الرفع مبتدأ.

143

As a rule the أَسْمـــاء الاسْتفهام have priority when starting a sentence (حَقُّ الصَّـــدَارَة). They may however be preceded by the مُضَافٌ or a الجَرِّ حُرُوفُ e.g.

Where is Zaid from?	مِنْ أَيْنَ زَيْدٌ ؟
Where is Aishah going?	إلى أين تَذْهَبُ عَائِشَةَ؟
Who are you calling?	بِمَنْ تَتَّصِلُ؟
Whose daughter is this?	إِبْنَةُ مَنْ هَذِه ؟
What is producing this sound?	صَوْتُ أَيِّ شَيْءٍ هَذَا ؟
Whose book did you read?	كِتَابُ مَنْ قَرَأتَ ؟

OVERVIEW

أدوات الاستفهام (12)

حروف(2)

أ ، هل

أسماء (10)

ما ، من ، ماذا
كيف ، متى ، أيّ ، كم
آيّان ، أنّى ، أين

IMPORTANT TERMS

أَسماء الاستفهام (1	The Interrogative nouns
مبتدأ مؤخر (2	The Delayed Subject
خبر مقدم (3	The Advanced Predicate
عاقل (4	Animate object
غير العاقل (5	Inanimate object

144

THE INTERROGATIVE NOUN

كم الاستفهام (6)	The Interrogative كم
كم الخبرية (7)	The Predicative كم

EXERCISE TWENTY

1) Use the following statements to make questions:

1) أدرس في الجامعة الإسلامية.

2) في جامعتنا ثلاثون طالبة مِن أفريقيا .

3) الطالبات يدخلن غرفة الدراسة بانتظام.

4) تتلقى الطالبات علومهنّ المفيدة نهارا.

5) يزورنا مدير المعهد كلّ أسبوع.

6) نحترم معلّمنا.

2) Specify the Interrogative nouns in the following sentences:

1) من منكنّ قرأت الدرس   2) كيف حال أبيك بعد خروجه من المستشفى ؟

3) ما هذا الفوضى ؟   4) هاتان بنتان , أيّهما أكبر؟

5) كم حاجا سافرا إلى مكة هذا العام؟   6) ما جاء بك اليوم ؟

7) أين دار عمك إبراهيم ؟   8) متى عطلة الصيف

9) كيف أصبحت ؟   10) ماذا تريد منّي؟

11) من أنبأك هذا؟   12) هل ينفع الحفظ بلا فهم

13) بنت من أنت ؟   14) من أين لك هذا

3) Analyse the following sentences:

2) أيّ درس نقرأ اليوم ؟   كيف حالك ؟

4) من حفظ الدرس ؟   رجعت من المدرسة ؟

6) كم عمرك ؟   ...ت ؟

145

4) Translate the following into English:

عن أبي هريرة رضي اللّه عنه قال: سمعت رسول الله صلى الله عليه وآله وسلم

يقول" :إنّ أوّل الناس يُقضى يوم القيامة عليه رجل استُشهد، فأُتي به فعرّفــــه

نعمه فعرفها، قال :فما عملت فيها؟ قال: قاتلت فيك حتى استشهدت، قـــال:

كذبت، ولكنّك قاتلت لأن يقال: جريءٌ. فقد قيل، ثمّ أُمر به فسُحب على

وجهه حتّى أُلقي في النار .ورجلٌ تعلّم العلم وعلّمه، وقرأ القرآن، فأتي بـــــه

فعرّفه نعمه فعرفها، قال: فما عملت فيها؟ قال: تعلّمت العلم وعلّمته، وقرأتُ

فيك القرآن، قال: كذبت، ولكنّك تعلّمت العلم ليقال: عالم، وقرأت القرآن

ليقال: هو قارئ، فقد قيل، ثمّ أمر به فسحب على وجهه حتى ألقي في النار .

ورجل وسّع الله عليه، وأعطاه من أصناف المال كلّه، فأتي به فعرّفـــــه نعمـــــه

فعرفها، قال: كذبت ، عملت فيها؟ قال: ما تركت من سبيل تحبّ أن يُنفق

فيها إلا أنفقت فيها لك ، قال: كذبت، ولكنك فعلت ليقال: هو جواد، فقد

قيل، ثمّ أمر به فسحب على وجهه، ثمّ ألقي في النار".

146

Chapter Twenty One

أَسْمَاءُ الشَّرْطِ

The Conditional Nouns

The *conditional nouns* are indeclinable nouns that govern two separate sentences to show that the implementation of the second sentences is linked to the implementation of the first. A sentence containing the conditional nouns is called الجُمْلَةُ الشَّرْطِيةُ or *the conditional sentence*. The first part is called جُمْلَةُ الشَّرْطِ and the second part is called جُمْلَةُ الجَوَابِ e.g.

Whosoever does evil will be punished for it.

مَنْ يَعْمَلْ سُوءاً يُجْزَ بِهِ

من : اسم الشرط مبني على السكون

يعمل : جملة الشرط

يجز به : جملة الجواب

Whatever good you do God is aware of it.

و مَا تَفْعَلُوا مِنْ خَيْرٍ يَعْلَمْهُ اللهُ

ما : اسم الشرط مبني على السكون

تفعلوا : جملة الشرط

الله : جملة الجواب

The conditional nouns are ten in number and are indeclinable apart from أيّ which is مُعْـــرَب. The conditional nouns are as follows:

مَنْ (ذو العقول)

Whosoever works hard will succeed.   مَنْ يَجْتَهِدْ يَنْجَحْ

مَا , مَهْمَا (غير ذو العقول)

Whatever you learn in young age will benefit you in old age   مَا تَتَعَلَّمْ فِي الصِّغَرِ يَنْفَعْكَ فِي الكِبَرِ

Whenever you order (me) to do good I will do it.   مَهْمَا تَأْمُرْ بِالخَيْرِ أَفْعَلْهُ

مَتَى , أَيَّانَ (الزمان)

When you die you will be well known.   مَتَى تَمُتْ تُعْرَفْ

Whenever you return you will meet me.   أَيَّانَ تَرْجِعْ تَلْقَنِي

كَيْفَمَا (حال)

In whatever situation you are so will be your partner.   كَيْفَمَا تَكُنْ يَكُنْ قَرِينُكَ

أَيْنَمَا , حَيْثُمَا , أَنَّى (مكان)

Where ever you are so death shall find you.   أَيْنَمَا تَكُونُوا يُدْرِكْكُمُ الْمَوْتُ

Whenever you go I will go.   حَيْثُمَا تَذْهَبْ أَذْهَبْ

Where ever you sit I will sit.   أَنَّى تَجْلِسْ أَجْلِسْ

أيّ (ذو العقول و غير ذو العقول)

whichever student works will pass.   أَيُّ طَالِبٍ يَجْتَهِدْ يَنْجَحْ

Whichever path you take so will I take.
أيُّ طَرِيقٍ تَسْلُكْ أَسْلُكْ

The conditional nouns govern both the شَرْطٌ and the جَوَابٌ in the conditional sentence making them *jussive* e.g.

مَنْ يَجْتَهِدْ يَنْجَحْ

من : اسم الشرط مبني على السكون

يجتهدْ : فعل مضارع مجزوم بمن , فعل الشرط

ينجحْ : فعل مضارع مجزوم بمن , جواب الشرط

The شَــــرْطٌ and جَوَابٌ are not always present tense verbs, they are also past tense, in such cases it will be فِي مَحَلٍّ الجَزْمِ e.g.

Whosoever performs the two "cold prayers" will enter paradise.
مَنْ صَلَّى البَرْدَيْنِ دَخَلَ الجَنَّةَ

من : اسم الشرط مبني على السكون

صلَّى : فعل ماض مبني على الفتحة في محل الجزم , فعل الشرط

دخل : فعل ماض مبني على الفتحة في محل الجزم , جواب الشرط

The شَرْطٌ and جَوَابٌ may also be in opposites tenses just as they can also be in past tense e.g.

من يجتهدْ نجحَ   مَنْ جَدَّ وَجَدَ   مَنْ اجْتَهَدَ يَنْجَحْ / يَنْجَحُ.

The جَوَابُ الشَّرْطِ may also be a nominal sentence, in which case it will be prefixed by the letter ف and will be فِي محل الجزم (*jussive*) e.g.

Whoever goes out in search of knowledge is in the path of God.
من خَرَجَ فِي طَلَبِ العِلْمِ فَهُوَ فِي سَبِيل الله

Whoever imitates a people will be considered as one of them.
شَبَّهَ بقومٍ فَهُوَ مِنْهُمْ

فهر : ضمير بارز منفصل مبني على الفتحة في محل الرفع مبتدأ

في سبيل الله : جار و مجرور شبه الجملة في محل الرفع خبر ,المبتدأ و الخبر

= جملة اسمية في محل الجزم, جواب الشرط

The above mentioned agents of condition (أَدَوَاتُ الشَّرْط) have a governing effect on the شرط and جواب. Thus they are termed أدواتُ الشرطِ الجازمة.

However, the conditional nouns are not the only agents of conditional sentences, some conditional sentences are introduced by *particles* which also have conditional meanings. These particles have no effect of جزم and are called أدواتُ الشَّرْطِ غَيْرِ الْجَازِمَةِ . They are as follows:

If Khalil was hardworking he would succeed.	لَوْ : لَوْ كَانَ خَلِيلٌ مُجتَهداً لَنَجَحَ
If it was not for the mercy of God people would perish.	لَوْلاَ : لَوْلاَ رَحْمَةُ الله لَهَلَكَ النَّاسُ
When God desires good for His servant He keeps him steadfast on obedience.	إذَا : إذَا أَرَادَ اللهُ بِعَبْدٍ خَيْراً أَلْزَمَهُ الطَّاعَةَ
Whenever Zakariya came in upon her in the *mihrab* he found her with nourishment.	كُلَّمَا : كُلَّمَا دَخَلَ عَلَيْهَا زَكَرِيَا الْمِحْرَابَ وَجَدَ عِنْدَهَا رزقا
When a Book came unto them from God they disbelieved in it.	لَمَّا : لَمَّا جَاءَهُمْ كِتَابٌ مِنْ عِنْدِ الله كَفَرُوا بِهِ

The procedure when analysing conditional sentences is as follows:

من ، ما ، مهما (ذو العقول و غير ذو العقول)

150

١) في محل الرفع مبتدأ ، يَليهِ فعل لازم أو فعل متعد ذُكِرَ مفعوله

٢) في محل النصب مفعول مقدم ، يليه فعل متعد لم يُذْكَرْ مفعوله

<u>مَنْ يجتهِدْ ينجحْ</u>

مَن : اسم الشرط مبني على السكون في محل الرفع مبتدأ

يجتهد : فعل مضارع مجزوم ، فعل الشرط ، و الفاعل ضمير مستتر هو

ينجح : فعل مضارع مجزوم ، جواب الشرط، والفاعل ضمير مستترهو.

و الجملة الشرطية المؤلفة من شرط و جوابه في محل الرفع ، خبر من.

<u>مَن يتّق اللهَ يَجْعَلْ لَهُ مَخْرَجاً</u>

مَن : اسم الشرط مبني على السكون في محل الرفع مبتدأ

يتّق : فعل مضارع مجزوم ، فعل الشرط ، و الفاعل ضمير مستتر هو.

الله : لفظ الجلالة منصوب ، مفعول به

يجعل: فعل مضارع مجزوم ، جواب الشرط ، و الفاعل ضمير مستتر
هو.له مخرجا : الجار و المجرور متعلق بالفعل ،

مخرجا : مفعول به منصوب. و الجملة الشرطية في محل الرفع ، خبر من.

<u>مَا تَفْعَلُوا مِنْ خَيْرٍ يَعْلَمْهُ اللهُ</u>

ما : اسم الشرط مبني على السكون في محل النصب مفعول مقدم

تفعلوا : فعل مضارع مجزوم ، فعل الشرط ، و الفاعل واو الجَمْعِ.

من خير : جار و مجرور متعلق بالفعل تفعلوا

يعلمه الله : فعل مضارع مجزوم ، جواب الشرط ، و الهاء ضمير بارز
متصل مبني على الضمة في محل النصب مفعول مقدم ،

الله : لفظ الجلالة فاعل مؤخر مرفوع.

151

مَهْما أَرَدْتَّ فَإِنِّي مُسْتَعِدٌّ لِقَضائِهِ.

مهما : ١ م الشرط مبني على السكون في محل النصب ، مفعول مقدم

أردت : فعل ماضٍ مبني على السكون في محل الجزم ، فعل الشرط ، و التاء تاء الفاعل

فإنّي مستعد لقضائه : جملة اسمية في محل الجزم جواب الشرط

<u>مَتَى ، أيَّان (الزمان)</u>

1)في محل النصب مفعول فيه (ظرف الزمان)

مَتَى تَذْهَبْ أذْهَبْ

متى : اسم الشرط مبني على السكون في محل النصب مفعول فيه (ظرف الزمان)

أيَّانَ تَزُرْني أُكْرِمْكَ

أيان : اسم الشرط مبني على السكون في محل النصب مفعول فيه (ظرف الزمان)

<u>أينما ، حيثما ، أنَّى (المكان)</u>

1) في محل النصب مفعول فيه

أيْنَمَا تَجْلِسْ أجْلِسْ

أينما : أسم الشرط مبنى على السكون في محل النصب مفعول فيه (ظرف المكان)

حَيْثُمَا تَسْكُنْ أسْكُنْ

حيثما: أسم الشرط مبنى على السكون في محل النصب مفعول فيه (ظرف المكان)

أنَّى تُسَافِرْ أسَافِرْ

أنَّى : أسم الشرط مبني على السكون في محل النصب مفعول فيه (ظرف

كيفما (حال)

1) في محل النصب حال

كَيْفَمَا تَكْتُبْ أَكْتُبْ

كيفما: أسم الشرط مبني على السكون في محل النصب حال

SUMMARY

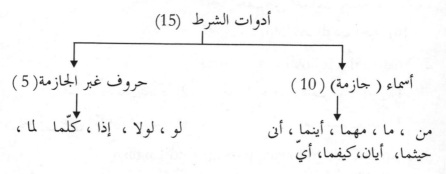

IMPORTANT TERMS

1) أسماء الشرط	The Conditional nouns	
2) الجملة الشرطية	The Conditional sentence	
3) جملة الشرط	The Conditional clause	
4) جملة الجواب	The Reply to the Condition	
5) أدوات الشرط الجازمة	The Jussive Agents of Condition	
6) أدوات الشرط غير الجازمة	The Non-Jussive Agents of Condition	

EXERCISE TWENTY ONE

1. Identify the شرط and جواب in the following sentences:

1) مهما تُنْفِقْ في الخير يُخْلِفْهُ الله

2) أنى ينزلْ ذو العلم يُكرمْ

3) أيّ بستان تدخلْ تبتهجْ

4) حيثما يتزلْ مطر ينمُ الزرعُ

5) كيفما نعاملْ صديقَك يعاملْك

6) من يحذرْ من عدوّه ينجُ من أذاه

7) متى يأتْ فصل الصيف يرحلْ الناس إلى الشاطئ

8) أينما تذهبْ أصحبْك

9) ما تُخفِ من أعمالِك يعلمْه الله

10) أيان يناد المؤذّن أجبْه

2) Analyse the following sentences:

1) أيّ طالب يجتهد ينجح   2) ما تضيع من وقتك تندم عليه

3) من صمت نجا   4) من يتوكل على الله فهو حسبه

3) Translate the following passage into English:

تكلّم أبو بكر رضي الله عنه بعد أن بَايَعَه الناسُ بالخلافة فَحَمِدَ اللّه وأَثْنَى عليه بالذي هو أَهْلُه ثم قال: أما بعدُ، أيُّها الناسُ فَإني قد وُلِّيتُ عليكــــم ولستُ بخيركم فإنْ أَحْسَنْتُ فَأَعِينُوني وإنْ أَسَأْتُ فَقَوِّمُوني. الصِّدقُ أمانةٌ والكَــــذِبُ خِيَانةٌ . والضعيفُ فيكم قوي عندي حتى أرجعَ إليه حقّه إن شاء اللّه، والقويّ فيكم ضعيفٌ عندي حتى آخذَ الحقّ منه إن شاء اللّه. لا يَدَعُ قومٌ الجِــــهادَ في سبيل اللّه إلا خَذَلَهم اللّهُ بالذُلِّ ولا تَشِيعُ الفاحشةُ في قوم إلا عَمَّــهم اللّــهُ بالبلاء. أطيعُوني ما أطَعْتُ اللّهَ ورسولَه فإذا عَصَيْتُ اللّهَ ورسولَه فلا طاعةَ لي عليكَم. قُومُوا إلى صلاتكم يَرْحَمْكُمُ اللّهُ.

Chapter Twenty Two

عَلاَمَاتُ الإعْرَابِ

The Signs of Declension

The Vowels ——— ٰ ٰ , as well as the anti-vowel ——— ْ when they appear over the last letter of a word indicate the *end-case* (إعْرَابٌ) of the word and they are called عَلاَمَاتُ الإعْـــرَاب or the signs of declension. These vowels are regarded as original signs (عَلاَمَات أصْلِيَّــــــةٌ). If you remember, in chapter three we said that a nominative word is a word that ends with a ضَمَّـةٌ "or its representatives", and an accusative words is a words that ends with فَتْحَـةٌ "or its representatives", etc. In chapter six we showed how the nouns in dual and plural forms change their end cases. You must have already concluded then that apart from the *original signs* of declension there are other signs used in other forms of nouns. Such signs are *substitute signs* (عَلاَمَات فَرْعِيَّةٌ). The signs of declension are thus of two types:

a) عَلاَمَاتُ الإعْرَابِ الأصْلِيَّةٌ Original signs of declension

b) عَلاَمَاتُ الإعْرَابِ الفَرْعِيَّةٌ Substitute signs of declension e.g.

The boy came. (nominative, *original sign*) جَاءَ الوَلَدُ

الوَلَد : فاعل مرفوع , و علامة الرفع الضمة الظاهرة

I saw the boy. (accusative, *original sign*) رَأَيْتُ الوَلَدَ

الوَلَد : مفعول به منصوب ، و علامة النصب الفتحة الظاهرة

The book is for the boy. (genitive, *original sign*) الكِتَابُ لِلْوَلَدِ

الولد : اسم مجرور باللام ، و علامة الجر الكسرة الظاهرة

The two boys came. (nominative, *substitute sign*) جَاءَ الوَلَدَان

الوَلَدَان : فاعل مرفوع ، و علامة الرفع الألف

I saw the two boys. (accusative. *substitute sign*) رأيت الوَلدَيْن

الوَلدَين : مفعول به منصوب ، و علامة النصب الياء

جاء المسلمُونَ

المسلمون : فاعل مرفوع ، و علامة الرفع الواو

The ضمَّة is an original sign of رفعٌ and serves as a nominative sign in the following instances:

1) الاسم المفرد

حضر المعلِّمُ

المَعلِّمُ : فاعل مرفوع ، و علامة الرفع الضمة الظاهرة

2) الجمع المكسّر

الأولادُ في الفصل

الأوْلاَدُ : مبتدأ المرفوع ، و علامة الرفع الضمة الظاهرة

3) جمع المؤنث السالم

حضرت المعلِّماتُ

المُعَلِّمَاتُ : فاعل مرفوع ، و علامة الرفع الضمة الظاهرة

4) الفعل المضارع المرفوع الصحيح

يذهبُ الطلاب إلى المسجد

يَذْهَبُ : فعل مضارع مرفوع ، و علامة الرفع الضمة الظاهرة

156

علامات الرفع الفرعية
Substitute nominative signs

The following signs substitute the ضمّة as nominative signs in the following instances:

1) لاسم المثنى:

قُتِلَ الرجلان

الرَّجُلانِ : نائب الفاعل مرفوع ، و علامة الرفع الألف لأنه مثنى

2) جمع المذكر السالم

كان المعلّمون حاضرين

الْمُعَلِّمُونَ : أسم كان مرفوع، و علامة الرفع الواو لأنه جمع مذكرسالم

3) الأفعال الخمسة (يذهبان – يذهبون – تذهبان – تذهبون–تذهبين)

الولدان يذهبان: فعل مضارع مرفوع و علامة الرفع ثبوت النون لأنه من الأفعال الخمسة

علامات النصب الأصلية
Original accusative signs

The *fatha* is an original sign of نَصبٌ, it serves as an accusative sign in the following instances:

1) الاسم المفرد

رأيت المعلّمَ : مفعول به منصوب ، و علامة النصب الفتحة الظاهرة

2) الجمع المكسّر

إنَّ الطلابَ مجتهدون : اسم ان منصوب ، و علامة النصب الفتحة الظاهرة.

157

٤) الفعل المضارع المنصوب الصحيح

لَنْ أذهبَ إلى السوق اليوم : فعل مضارع منصوب بِلَنْ ، و علامة النصب الفتحة الظاهرة.

علامات النصب الفرعية

Substitute accusative signs

The following signs substitute the *fatha* as accusative signs in the following cases:

١) الاسم المفرد

كان الطالبان مجتهدَين : خبركان منصوب وعلامة النصب الياءلأنه مثني

٢) جمع المذكر السالم

رأيتُ المعلّمِينَ : مفعول به منصوب ، وعلامة النصب الياء لأنه جمع مذكر سالم

٣)جمع المؤنث السالم

رأيت المسلمات : مفعول به منصوب و علامة النصب الكسرة الظاهرة لأنه جمع مؤنث سالم

٤) الأفعال الخمسة (يذهبان – يذهبون – تذهبان – تذهبون – تذهبين)

الولدان لَنْ يَذْهَبَا : فعل مضارع منصوب بلن و علامة النصب حذف النون لأنه من الأفعال الخمسة

علامات الجرّ الأصلية
Original genitive signs

The *kasra* is an original sign of جرّ it serves as a genitive sign in the following instances:

١) الاسم المفرد

ذهبتُ إلى المسجدِ : اسم مجرور بإلى، و علامة الجرِّ الكسرة الظاهرة

٢) الجمع المكسّر

الطلاب في الفصول : اسم مجرور بفي، و علامة الجرّ الكسرة الظاهرة

٣) جمع المؤنث السالم

الدفاتر للطالبات : اسم مجرور بللام ، و علامة الجرّ الكسرة الظاهرة

علامات الجرّ الفرعية
Substitute genitive signs

The following signs substitute the *kasra* as genitive signs in the following instances:

١-الاسم المثني

برُّ الوالدَين واجبٌ : مضاف إليه مجرور و علامة الجرّ الياء لأنه مثني

٢) جمع مذكر سالم

الإسلامُ دينُ المسلمِينَ : مضاف إليه مجرور و علامة الجرّ الياء لأنه جمع
مذكر سالم

٣) الاسم ممنوع من الصرف

رجع خالد من مكةَ : اسم مجرور بمن و علامة الجرّ الفتحة لأنه ممنوع
من الصرف

علامات الجزم الأصلية

Original Jussive signs

The *sukun* is an original sign of جزم , it serves as a jussive sign in the following instances:

١- الفعل المضارع المجزوم

عليٌّ لَمْ يذهبْ إلى السوق: فعل مضارع مجزوم وعلامة الجزم السكون

علامات الجزم الفرعية

Substitute jussive signs

The following signs substitute the *sukun* as the jussive signs in the following instances:

١) الأفعال الخمسة

أنتم لَمْ تذهبوا :

فعل مضارع مجزوم و علامة الجزم حذف النون لأنه من الأفعال الخمسة

٢) الفعل المضارع المعتل الآخر

لَمْ يرمِ خالد الكرة :

فعل المضارع مجزوم بلم، وعلامة الجزم حذف حرف العلّة لأنه معتل الآخر

الإعْرَابُ الظَّاهِرُ و المُقَدَّرُ

Implicit and explicit declension

Some words have no apparent sign showing the end-case. In such cases the sign is *implicit* (مُقَدَّرٌ). When the sign is clear and apparent it is called ظَـاهِرٌ. The مُقَدَّرٌ signs are found in the following types of words:

1) الاسم المقصور

جاء الفَتَى (ضمة مقدّرة) – رأيت الفتَى (فتحة مقدّرة) – الكتاب لِلْفَتَى (كسرة مقدّرة)

جاء الفتى : فاعل مرفوع و علامة الرفع الضمة المقدّرة على الألف لأنه مقصور

2) الاسم المنقوص (جاء القَاضِيْ – الكِتَابُ عِنْدَ القَاضِيْ)

جاء القاضي : فاعل مرفوع و علامة الرفع الضمة المقدّرة على اليـــاء لأنه منقوص

الكتاب عند القاضي : مضاف إليه مجرور و علامة الجرّ الكسرة المقدّرة على الياء لأنه منقوص

رأيتُ القَاضِيَ : مفعول به منصوب و علامة النصب الفتحة الظاهرة

3) الفعل المضارع المعتل الآخر

خالد يَدعُو : فعل مضارع مرفوع و علامة الرفع الضمة المقدّرة علـــى آخره لأنه معتل الآخر

حامد يَجري : فعل مضارع مرفوع و علامة الرفع الضمة المقـــدّرة على آخره لأنه معتل الآخر

لا أخْشَى الفقر : فعل مضارع مرفوع و علامة الرفع الضمة المقـــدّرة على آخره لأنه معتل الآخر

لن أخْشَى الفقر : فعل مضارع منصوب بلن و علامة النصب_ الفتحة المقدّرة على آخره لأنه معتل الآخر

IMPORTANT TERMS

1)	علامات الإعراب	The Signs of declension
2)	علامات أصلية	Original signs
3)	علامات فرعية	Substitute signs
4)	إعراب ظاهر	Apparent signs of declension
5)	إعراب مقدّر	Supposed signs of declension

EXERCISE TWENTY TWO

1) State the signs of declension in the underlined words and the reason where possible:

١- البستان لم يثمر

٢- لا تنس ذكر الله

٣- ان المسلمات صالحات

٤- ذهب أبي إلى مصر

٥- خرجت الطبيب من المستشفي

٦- سافر التاجران إلى القدس

٧- كان الأولاد مجتهدين

٨- لا ندعو إلى الشر

٩- حكم القاضي في القضيّة

١٠- الطلاّب لم يخرج من قاعة الامتحان بعد

١١- أكلت التفّاحتين

12- حضر مديرُ المدرسة

13- جاء أبو سعيد

14- رأيتَ أبا سعيد

15- رضي الناس عن أبي سعيد

2) Translate the following passage:

خطبة طارقِ بنِ زيادٍ رحمه اللّه تعالى:

قام طارق بن زياد خطيباً في أصحابه، فحَمِدَ اللّه وأثنى عليه بما هو أهله ثم حثّ المسلمين على الجهاد ورغّبهم ثم قال: أيها الناس، أين المَفَرُّ؟ البحرُ مِـــن ورائكم، والعدوُّ أمامَكم وليس لكم واللّهِ إلا الصدقُ والصَبْرُ. واعلموا أنكـــم في هذه الجزيرة أضْيَعُ من الأيتام في مَأْدُبَةِ اللِّئام، وقد استقْبَلَكم عدوّكم بجَيْشِهِ وأسلِحَتِهِ، وأقواتُه موفورةٌ ، وأنتم لا وَزَرَ لكم إلا سيوفُكم ولا أقوات إلا ما تَسْتَخْلِصُونَه من أيدِي عدوِّكم، وإن امْتَدَّتْ بكم الأيامُ على افتقـــاركم و لم تُنْجزوا لكم أمراً ذهبتْ ريحُكم، و تَعَوَّضَتِ القلوبُ من رُعْبها منكم الجَرَاءَ ة عليكم، فادفعوا عن أنفسكم خُذْلانَ هذه العاقبة من أمركم بمُنَـــاجَزَةِ هـــذا الطاغية.

163

Goodword English Publications

The Holy Quran: Text, Translation and Commentary (HB), Tr. Abdullah Yusuf Ali

The Holy Quran (PB), Tr. Abdullah Yusuf Ali

The Holy Quran (Laminated Board), Tr. Abdullah Yusuf Ali

The Holy Quran (HB), Tr. Abdullah Yusuf Ali

Holy Quran (Small Size), Tr. Abdullah Yusuf Ali

The Quran, Tr. T.B. Irving

The Koran, Tr. M.H. Shakir

The Glorious Quran, Tr. M.M. Pickthall

Allah is Known Through Reason, Harun Yahya

The Basic Concepts in the Quran, Harun Yahya

Crude Understanding of Disbelief, Harun Yahya

Darwinism Refuted, Harun Yahya

Death Resurrection Hell, Harun Yahya

Devoted to Allah, Harun Yahya

Eternity Has Already Begun, Harun Yahya

Ever Thought About the Truth?, Harun Yahya

The Mercy of Believers, Harun Yahya

The Miracle in the Ant, Harun Yahya

The Miracle in the Immune System, Harun Yahya

The Miracle of Man's Creation, Harun Yahya

The Miracle of Hormones, Harun Yahya

The Miracle in the Spider, Harun Yahya

The Miracle of Creation in DNA, Harun Yahya

The Miracle of Creation in Plants, Harun Yahya

The Moral Values of the Quran, Harun Yahya

The Nightmare of Disbelief, Harun Yahya

Perfected Faith, Harun Yahya